State and Nation in the Third World

The Western State and African Nationalism

Anthony D. Smith

Senior Lecturer in Sociology,
London School of Economics and Political Science

A MEMBER OF THE HARVESTER PRESS GROUP

First published in Great Britain in 1983 by
WHEATSHEAF BOOKS LTD
A MEMBER OF THE HARVESTER PRESS GROUP
Publisher: John Spiers
Director of Publications: Edward Elgar
16 Ship Street, Brighton, Sussex

© Anthony D. Smith 1983

British Library Cataloguing in Publication Data

Smith, Anthony D.
    State and nation in the Third World.
    1. Africa, Sub-Saharan—Social conditions—1960-
    2. Africa, Sub-Saharan—Politics and government
    —1960-
    I. Title
    967   DT352

ISBN 0-7108-0199-8 cloth
ISBN 0-7108-0189-0 pbk

Photoset in 11/12 pt Bembo by P.R.G. Graphics Ltd,
Redhill, Surrey.
Printed in Great Britain by St Edmundsbury Press Ltd,
Bury St Edmunds, Suffolk

Contents

Preface   vii

1   The Western Model   1

2   Imperialism and Colonialism   18

3   Nationalism in Africa   37

4   Ethnicity and Class   59

5   State and Intelligentsia   79

6   Populism and Communism   97

7   Forging Territorial Nations   122

Notes   137

Bibliography   147

Index of Names   163

Index of Subjects   169

Preface

My aim in the present work is to explore the nature and role of some key political forces in contemporary social change in Africa and Asia, and especially in sub–Saharan Africa. In both continents the historic confrontation of Western political institutions with indigenous social structures, economies and cultures has provided the basic framework for their social and economic development (or lack of it) in recent decades. At the centre of current transformations in the countries of Africa and Asia has been a more or less conscious effort to create 'territorial nations' within the historical framework of western-imposed bureaucratic states, by a political intelligentsia to whose needs and interests the postcolonial state-nations minister. This undertaking helps to explain many of these states' social and political problems today. Under the influence of the dominant modernisation and marxist paradigms, most accounts fail to give these essentially political processes enough attention and thereby accord too little weight to an autonomous political sector, which they tend to derive from either basic economic forces or overarching cultural values. My aim therefore is to complement their accounts by analysing the *political* dimensions they so often neglect or relegate. In no way do I seek to provide an overall survey of social change in Africa and Asia, let alone an exhaustive analysis of recent literature on the subject, something that would require more than a single volume.

To illustrate my thesis I have drawn on examples mainly from sub–Saharan Africa, with which I am most familiar. But several of the arguments may also apply, *mutatis mutandis*, to Asian countries, though some of them are economically more advanced than their African counterparts. I think that the Latin American case is rather different and have therefore not sought to draw any parallels. In this, as in other cases, it seems preferable to observe the fundamental cultural and historical

Preface

differences. And if such a 'partial' account with its predominantly political emphasis helps to stimulate further discussion of the issues it seeks to address, it will have achieved its exploratory aims.

Anthony D. Smith.
London, June 1982.

1 The Western Model

This book aims to develop some general arguments about the formation and role of states and nations, and their ruling strata, in non-European societies, notably in sub-Saharan Africa, in the light of West European experiences. Throughout the world, economic growth and social change have taken place within very varied political and cultural contexts, and hence such apparently uniform developments as technological advance, rising material standards and output, rapid urbanisation, the commercialisation of agriculture, the redistribution of wealth and the provision of a wider range of social services for the population, take on a different significance and have different consequences according to this political and cultural context. Three elements of this context stand out in recent history and form a set of common threads in an otherwise highly heterogeneous picture of contemporary social changes: the rise of the modern state, the emergence of national communities and of nationalist ideologies and sentiments, and the formation of new strata, notably bureaucrats, bourgeoisies and intelligentsia. Together these common elements, though differing in their relative weight and significance, afford a basis for comparing societies and cultures with otherwise quite distinctive patterns of thought and behaviour.

It might be asked why we should follow the tradition of taking the Western experience as a baseline for comparisons with African and Asian developments. Several reasons suggest themselves for such a procedure. In the first place, and most obviously, it was in Western Europe that the three elements I have selected, made their first appearance; and secondly, it was through the agency of these same Europeans that these elements were transported and transplanted into their non-European settings, though with considerable change in content and quite different consequences. Today, too, the leaders of African and Asian states implicitly, if not openly, make the selfsame comparisons, and seek to model their political and, to some extent, their cultural institutions and styles on Western forms: and *form*, the modes and procedures through which experiences are channelled and realised, exercises a continuous influence on the contents of those experiences.

Issues of theory and method also invite comparisons with Western experience. Social science aims to develop concepts and models which are not culture-bound, as tools for elucidating different patterns of culture and society; and hence cross-cultural comparisons, such as those between African and Western states, may help us refine these tools. Provided, moreover, that the Western point of departure is not allowed to influence the analysis unduly, (and avoids therefore the use of too general 'ideal types' drawn from Western history), the use of more specific concepts and models may allow us to see the Western experience itself in a new light, and to question the underlying evolutionary assumptions common to much theoretical enquiry in this field. It is that theoretical heritage centred as it is on comparisons with the Western experience, which requires us to reconsider those fundamental assumptions, exactly because of its relative failure to give an adequate account of the political and cultural sectors, and especially the issues of state formation, nationalism and the ruling strata, which play so vital a part in both economic growth and social development.

Broadly speaking, we can distinguish two dominant approaches in that theoretical heritage. The first posits a more or less universal 'transition' from a feudal mode of production and social structure to a capitalist one in the West, and an analogous process of development in non-Western societies, from a variety of 'pre-capitalist' (or better, 'non-capitalist') modes to either a capitalist, or a dependent or peripheral capitalist, society and mode of production.[1] Within this general approach, we must also distinguish a variety of more specific theories and perspectives, and a growing recognition of the role played by exogenous forces, notably the world economy.[2] I shall return to consider some of these perspectives in the next chapter.

The other dominant approach also posits a universal development, but this time from a 'traditional' type of society, economy and culture, to one that is 'modern' in its main features, and it assumes that the process of 'modernisation' by which this transition is effected, possesses an underlying pattern common to all cases, although local conditions will tend to modify the pace, timing, intensity and scope of this process.[3] Here, too, we need to distinguish a variety of sub-approaches and specific theories, of which undoubtedly the best-known and most influential have been a type of western diffusionism of values and techniques, centred on Parsons' schema of 'pattern-variables', and the related but more rigorously theoretical 'neo-evolutionism' adopted by the later Parsons, and particularly by Smelser, Levy and Bellah.[4] For the most part, this kind of approach has been pitched at so general a level, that it offers very little illumination of just those specific political and cultural issues that interest us here; and for this reason, I propose to concentrate rather on those other perspectives which have something valuable to say about these questions.

Before turning to these other approaches, however, I want to say something about two variants of the modernisation approach, advanced by social scientists more or less associated with the 'neo-evolutionist' perspective. Edward Shils was among the earliest theorists to stress the role of elites, and especially the ideological intelligentsia, in the political development of the new states.[5] He has drawn attention to the various kinds of political strategy of development, and related them to different kinds of elites who have adopted competing ideologies to legitimate sweeping social changes; and showed early on how the varieties of nationalist and socialist programmes involved an ethic of self-purification and regeneration by an intelligentsia torn between different worlds of discourse and clashing outlooks. Indeed, the conflict between a westernising and an indigenous nativist commitment and outlook forms one of the matrices of the problems of the intelligentsia, and by extension, of the political formation of many new states in Africa and Asia, notably India.[6] Shils' analysis rightly fastens on the crucial role of the intelligentsia in the new states, a theme to which I shall return later; yet, in keeping with much modernisation theory, his understanding of the basic processes of contemporary change in the 'Third World', the fundamental notions of 'development' and 'modernisation' that he employs, are impregnated with Western cultural assumptions (so that 'modernisation' is blurred with its twin, 'westernisation') and the different kinds of 'political development' in non-Western states are measured by Western standards, to the relative neglect of a causal analysis at the local and inter-state levels.

Eisenstadt, too, has sought to account for the variety of routes towards 'modernity' in terms of different kinds of elites, as well as the timing of entry into the 'modernisation process'.[7] These elites in fact create the mechanisms of political integration, as well as the particular strategies, which provide the framework and instruments for a successful bid for modernisation. Eisenstadt clearly recognises the exogenous nature of the process of modernisation outside the West, as well as the important role of intelligentsia; it is these elites who channel and 'refract' the forces of modernisation emanating from the West, as well as the ensuing pressures of the peripheral areas of a state on its centre. In other words, elites become 'managers of modernisation'. They organise the social mobilisation of the masses who press for greater participation in decision-making at the centre, and particularly in political and bureaucratic organs. Essential, therefore, to this process of modernisation, defined here as the trend towards mass participation at the centre, is the need to build strong institutions which are no longer guided by traditional codes and symbols, but which incorporate a large measure of rational conduct based on ideals of universalism and equality.[8] In singling out the 'political centre' as the arena and locus of modernisation, Eisenstadt ties his analysis of elite roles to the first of our three areas of interest, the formation of the modern state. Moreover, Eisenstadt is one of the very few 'modernisation' theorists to place the processes of economic growth and social development (in the sense of greater social equality and provision of welfare services for all) within a broader context of political and cultural change, even if he still remains within the general orbit of 'neo-evolutionist' schemas with their heavy endogenous bias.[9]

Several other schemes of 'political development' devote some attention to our three problems, notably the analyses of Almond and Apter and Binder, who have attempted to distinguish different kinds of political structures and ideologies relevant to 'modernisation' processes.[10] Curiously, however, they have not taken any of our issues as their central problematic, although Binder and others have devoted considerable attention to different forms of nationalist ideology and sentiment in the Middle East and Africa, and have been sensitive to the constraints placed upon local change by developments at the international level. Their functional approach, however, to the role of the ideology, with nationalism often being viewed as a form of 'political religion', has tended to inhibit a more historical–causal analysis of the rise of nationalist movements and ideologies within the framework of colonial territories: with the result that current political and social structures assume the status of 'givens' of historically necessary outcomes − as they appeared to be in the West.[11]

This 'western' bias also pervades that sub-variety of 'modernisation' theory which *does* accord a central role to processes of 'nation-building', namely, the 'communications' model associated with Karl Deutsch and Daniel Lerner. Both writers are interested in charting the processes which lead to the formation of nations. Both are also essentially interested in a 'western' process of development, and in Deutsch's case with actual Western examples. And both find in the process of 'social mobilisation' the key to that process.

Of the two, Lerner's scheme is less complex, more psychologistic. It attempts to explain the patterns of development, mainly in the Middle East, as part of a universal movement from closed, localised, traditional communities to open, mobile and participant, national societies, a movement which is rarely smooth or uninterrupted, but usually full of false starts, diversions and painful bottlenecks, a period or stage which Lerner labels 'transitional'.[12] It is in this transitional phase that the social mechanisms and personality traits appear which, for all the temporary distortions along the way, allow populations and states to forsake traditionalism for the high plateau of modernity. And we can measure this movement towards the end-state of modernity by the extent of development along key interrelated dimensions, notably those of urbanisation, literacy, exposure to mass media and political participation: in Lerner's own words:

Everywhere, for example, increasing urbanisation has tended to raise literacy; rising literacy has tended to increase media exposure; increasing media exposure has 'gone with' wider economic participation (per capita income) and political participation (voting).[13]

Undoubtedly, the most important of the social mechanisms is mobility, both geographical and social. Given a sufficient degree of mobility, and particularly urbanisation, all the other indices of modernisation will come into play and reinforce each others' cumulative effect — as they did in the West. But, even more vital, they will also induce psychic mobility. The mass media, in particular, will 'multiply mobility' within the personality structure by expanding the range of situations in which a man or woman can imagine him/herself and the number of identifications a person can make. In other words, the mass media magnify the capacity for 'empathy', 'the capacity to see oneself in the other fellow's situation'.[14] Empathy encourages the growth of mobile personalities, which are essential to the smooth functioning of modern participant societies. This is because empathy involves a desire for change and innovation, and the latter are important constituents of modernisation. On the other hand, empathy can never be the sole motor of modernisation; the latter also depends on the prior mobilisation of individuals out of their traditional settings:

. . . the media spread psychic mobility most efficiently among peoples who have in some measure achieved the antecedent conditions of geographic and social mobility.[15]

What, then, for Lerner, is the end-product of social mobilisation and modernisation? The participant society at the end of the road is really a nation-state with a fairly homogeneous, if flexible, national culture; and the rise of these end-forms of modernisation in Lerner's account turns out to be an analytic re-description of the basic processes of the 'Western' route to modernity. Indeed, the nation-state and its national culture is the only possible framework for that modernity. Unfortunately, to reach the threshold of modernity, peoples must negotiate the painful, disturbing straits of national*ism*, with its frenetic rejection of the West and simultaneous embrace of all things western. For, in that limbo of transition to modernity, the newly mobile personalities are filled with ambivalent longings, which find expression in the regrettable but temporary necessity of nationalism. In the Middle East, especially, westernisation in a transitional society is inevitably accompanied by a frenzied xenophobia and anticolonialism, as social mobilisation and empathy erode the bases of Islamic culture and tradition.[16]

For all its naïve psychologism and diffusionism, Lerner's model does raise in acute form the major issues of the Western impact on states and populations in other continents. Two aspects of this impact are important here: its prescriptive appeal, and the channels through which it operates. As to the first of these aspects, Lerner's account is admittedly permeated by a rather crude ethnocentrism. It is simply not the case that the Western model 'reappears in virtually all modernising societies on all continents of the world, regardless of variations in race, colour, creed[17]' unless, of course, we equate 'modernising' with 'westernising'. Nor can we regard the view that the 'sequence of current events in the Middle East can be understood as a deviation, in some measure a deliberate deformation, of the Western model'[17] as anything but a gross simplification of contemporary social change in that area. Besides, doesn't such a formulation beg the question: can we really speak of a unified 'Western model'?

On the other hand, some measure of Western 'ethnocentrism' seems to be unavoidable. First, because a number (though by no means all) African and Asian leaderships advocate westernisation in some form or other; as Lerner puts it rather sweepingly,

. . . western society still provides the most developed model of societal attributes (power, wealth, skill, rationality) which Middle East spokesmen continue to advocate as their own goal. . . . What the West is, in this sense, the Middle East seeks to become.[18]

But, more importantly, because the allegedly 'universal' components of recent social change — industrial technology, economic growth, mass participation, the capitalist mode of production — cannot easily be disentangled from their 'western' conceptual and historical format and connotations. It was, after all, in the 'West' that all these processes emerged, and it was from the specific meanings of Western history and its cultural significance (in Weber's sense) that they derived their importance for us.[19] It was, furthermore, by an exogenous process of intrusion — whether we call it diffusion, importation, transplantation or penetration — that these and other processes first made their appearance in Asia and Africa, even though the local settings altered much of their content and significance. Even the overall framework in which each of these processes operates, the so-called 'nation-state', has been quite consciously modelled on Western political forms. Hence the normative and prescriptive appeal of this 'Western model' cannot be gainsaid.

With regard to the channels of this Western impact, also, Lerner's model points to one salient fact: that increasing contact with the West, that is, with a very different and technologically much more advanced culture, has fostered new aspirations and visions of change, has raised expectations which cannot be satisfied and thereby helped to increase social discontent and hostility, and has provided a language in which new ideals can be formulated to cater to the grievances and interests of incipient classes and competing ethnic communities — dimensions which more structuralist explanations sometimes overlook. Of course, 'communications' do not provide the sole channels of Western intrusion, nor can the mass media compete in importance with political and economic channels of penetration, which, in any case, usually dictate the 'messages of modernisation'. But 'communications theory' also serves to remind us that the Western impact is not confined to the sphere of economic imperialism and ensuing dependency; that the cultural (scientific, humanistic, ideological, educational) aspects of that intrusion have also been powerful agents of social change in Africa and Asia.[20]

A more sophisticated and complex variant of 'communications theory' is presented in the various writings of Karl Deutsch. Deutsch's specific interest is the formation of nations, based on what he calls 'ethnic complementarity'. He starts by providing a functional definition of nationality as consisting in 'wide complementarity of social communication':

It consists . . . in the ability to communicate more effectively, and over a wider range of subjects, with members of one large group than with outsiders.[21]

But social communications is not enough to form a community or nationality; economic intercourse, the mobility of goods and persons, is also vital. A 'nationality' comes, therefore, to mean

an alignment of large numbers of individuals from the middle and lower classes linked to regional centres and leading social groups by channels of social communication and economic intercourse, both indirectly from link to link and directly with the centre.[22]

A nationality becomes a 'nation' when it possesses an additional power to compel its members and back up group aspirations; a sovereign 'nation-state' is a nation that has successfully attained these aspirations, a nation with a new or old state organisation at its service, whose very power and success may thrust it into conflict with other claimant nationalities.

How, then, do nations and nationalities form? Basically, according to Deutsch, through the twin processes of cultural assimilation and social mobilisation. Technically, 'cultural assimilation' means that the same information fed to members of different groups exceeds the different stores of information which feed their respective group memories. In practice, this means that smaller, subordinate communities or nationalities are absorbed into the information and communications networks of the larger, dominant 'nations', as the Bretons tended to be absorbed into France and the Welsh in England, or European immigrants into American culture. Rapid assimilation occurred in France during the French Revolution and Britain during the Industrial Revolution, because in both periods there was an unprecedented increase in intensive social communications and economic and social opportunities. Where there was little or no revolution or immigration process, as among Slavs in Greece or Copts in Egypt, assimilation was slower. In all these cases, cultural minorities have adopted the language of the dominant majority — and language adoption is for Deutsch the main index of cultural assimilation — with the result that 'community' is growing faster than 'society'; that is to say, during a period of cultural assimilation, people will communicate more and faster than their working lives demand, and so become an assimilated population.

Cultural assimilation is usually accompanied by 'social mobilisation'. Deutsch defines the latter as the process by which men and women are uprooted from their traditional, agrarian settings as a result of social, economic and technical development, and are thereby 'mobilised' for more intensive communication. In this way, a 'public' is created. The best index of social mobilisation is provided by the rate of urbanisation; for, though there are other indices of mobilisation — literacy, taxation, conscription and voting, for example — they tend to operate within an urban context, and as effects of rapid urbanisation. Deutsch gives some examples of the different ways in which assimilation and mobilisation tend to produce nations: the development of Finland from 1750 to 1918, for instance, was characterised by gradual cultural assimilation to the Finnish tongue along with growing urbanisation both of Finns and in Sweden as a whole, at a time when Finland was simply a Swedish province with a dominant Swedish-speaking urban class. In Bohemia, on the other hand, the mobilisation of a Czech-speaking population (and assimilation to the Czech language) after 1800 brought in its train sharp conflicts with the Sudeten Germans, until the fortunes of the Second World War decided the issue.[23]

As these examples show, the fact of growing mobilisation and assimilation cannot predict the shape and emergence of *particular* national formations. But, for Deutsch, 'nation-building' is an essential component of development and modernisation. That is to say, from a methodological standpoint, the indices of 'modernisation' can be used to plot the growth of nations and nation-states; ideologically, 'nation-building' is part and parcel of the ideal of progress resulting from mobilisation and assimilation; while, theoretically, the processes of modernisation and communications are felt to 'explain' the growth of nations and nation-states, or at any rate of some nations and nation-states.[24]

Now, although Deutsch's approach is both general and global in scope, his examples are drawn mainly from the European experience, and, more important, reflect his profound knowledge of that heritage and the several factors that have gone into its peculiar outcome. For what has been peculiar about the European historical model is its selectivity: it has 'produced' *some* states and *some* nations (and a few real 'nation-states'), out of all the many candidates for statehood and nationhood that appeared on the continent in the last five centuries since both began to form.[25] This means that many possible states — Burgundy, Prussia, Savoy, Piedmont — and many potential nations — Saxons, Wends, Frisians, Vlachs — have 'failed' to maintain themselves or to develop into lasting 'building-blocks'. In Walker Connor's terms, 'nation-building' has entailed 'nation-destroying'; or, even better, 'state-building' has erased or eroded many a variable nation.[26] For, as we shall see, the Western model is essentially a 'state system' rather than a 'nation system'; and this has been its fateful legacy to Africa and Asia.

Of itself, this fact does not invalidate Deutsch's approach. Ideally, social mobilisation should proceed *pari passu* with cultural assimilation, in well-regulated steps, if a politically integrated nation-state is to emerge and survive. The difficulty is that such a sequence is very rare. It is based on the British, French and possibly Dutch and Spanish experiences; and, even in these cases, recent developments have cast considerable doubts on the efficacy of the twin processes to produce and sustain nations. It is quite possible to claim today that 'France' and 'Britain' refer solely to political entities, states which include several nations; though others might argue that we may legitimately speak of 'nations' containing, as it were, 'sub-nations'.[27] At any rate, the Franco-British experience is unique; its importance lies in its 'mythopoeic' qualities, the historically unique constellation that lent these states an appearance of cultural homogeneity at a crucial moment of time, when they were the dominant political and cultural models for so much of the world. Within Europe, the much more frequent sequence has been an excess of mobilisation to assimilation (a situation that Deutsch himself analysed), leading to growing cultural differences and eventually a reactive ethnic nationalism among the fully mobilised population who stress their separate cultural identity. That is what occurred in Eastern Europe with the failure of Russification or Germanisation policies in the last century; and the same phenomenon is reappearing today in Western Europe's plural states with their high rates of social mobilisation.[28] A similar sequence can be found in many parts of Africa and Asia. As urbanisation proceeds apace, as commerce and industry make inroads into the traditional agrarian economy, as educated publics are formed, so various ethnic groups begin to aspire to national status and even statehood. In so far as modernisation is at all responsible, it appears to be an agent of 'state-destroying' through cultural differentiation, rather than 'nation-building' through any cultural assimilation.

But we can go further and question the underlying assumption that 'modernisation' or 'development' is so closely tied to the rise of 'nations'. Of course, it all depends on how we define those elastic terms, 'modernisation' and 'development'. If we define them in terms of the various processes of 'social mobilisation' and especially urbanisation and industrialisation, then there is a rather loose sense in which mobilising people makes them 'available' as a public for concentrated action. But why should these publics form 'nations' or 'nation-states', as opposed to classes, occupational interest groups or purely geographical regions? Indeed, they often do — urbanisation, especially, provides a vital locus and framework for class formation. But cities, or even city-states, do not constitute 'nations'; and *their* heyday (ancient Greek city-states, medieval Italian city-republics, the Hanseatic League) actually militated against the formation of nation-states.[29] A nation-state certainly requires a capital (though it can be 'invented', as in Brazil or Australia), if only for symbolic reasons, and the growth of cities are indirect, if necessary, conditions of nation-formation; but they are never sufficient conditions, and both capitals and provincial centres are likely to throw up classes and occupational strata and unions more than 'nations'. On the other hand, the dominance of a capital is often an index and agent of 'state-formation', and of its ruling stratum.

As for cultural assimilation, and especially language adoption, neither need be linked with processes of 'modernisation'. Rather, they appear as partial indicators of the growth of nations, and even here, intermittently. In this respect, the European experience has not been replicated in all parts of Africa and Asia; even in Europe, Switzerland suggests that language homogeneity, though important, may not be overriding.[30] In fact, language in the strict sense is much more likely to divide populations and thwart communications networks in areas like India or sub-Saharan Africa, and so fragment them into the smallest descent groups above the immediate kin networks, in so far as it possesses any real

political force. With a *lingua franca* for elites, language differences need not impede a broader cultural homogenisation in
many African and Asian societies.[31]

More generally, we may say that the rise of particular networks of communications constitutes one important means of
operationalising the concept of a 'nation', and of charting the
transformation of populations into compact 'nations', provided we do not equate those networks with a vernacular in
the strict sense; for the effects of the latter are highly variable
for the growth of nations. Other cultural networks – religion,
customs, myths, folklore, art – must also be taken into
account; above all, the manner in which all these modes of
communication enshrine common and distinctive historical
memories, and the forces which endow these modes with life
and meaning, must be studied, if we are to gain a fuller picture
of the complex processes of nation-formation.

Deutsch's work, then, provides an important point of
departure for the study of nation-formation, especially in
Europe, in so far as it highlights some of the mechanisms of
nationality and opens up avenues for research into the processes of their creation. But it also suffers from a certain
Europocentrism and a tendency to assume an immediate,
unmediated link between modernisation and nation-forming.
Though conscious of the many historical routes to the growth
of nations, Deutsch underplays the importance of historical
events and crises, the sense of contingency and of the con-
fluence of various historical chains, that went into the processes of nation-formation in Europe and outside. And it is
exactly these historical dimensions and specific sequences that
various scholars, influenced by Deutsch's general approach,
have sought to introduce into his model, with important
results for the study of similar processes outside Europe.

In an important volume devoted to the rise of nation-states
in Western Europe, Charles Tilly and his colleagues attempt to
trace the conditions and processes which brought certain
nation-states into being and ensured their maintenance, at the
cost of many other candidates, from 1500 to the 19th
century.[32] Actually, as Tilly makes clear, the formation of
states is the real object of their several investigations. As Tilly
observes, the rise of nations, in Western Europe at any rate,

occurred *after* the era of absolute monarchies and was largely the product of the consolidation of these powerful centralised states. By the modern 'state' Tilly refers to a territorially well-defined unit, with a relatively centralised, autonomous and differentiated set of governmental institutions with a monopoly over (and concentration of) the means of physical coercion within that territory.[33] The national state, moreover, is sovereign in the double sense, that its governmental institutions claim total independence of other internal institutions, and brook no rivals within its territorial domain, and that they claim complete independence of other analogous governmental institutions, or states, outside the particular territory. At any rate, this was the pattern of political unit that began to emerge from the 15th century onwards, until it became the norm in Europe during the later 19th and early 20th centuries. Moreover, the earlier process of 'state-building', often undertaken in the teeth of internal opposition and moulded in the fires of intense warfare, provided the framework for the growth of 'nations', in the sense of culturally homogeneous, territorially compact and economically unified 'political communities' of destiny, even though to this day 'states' and 'nations' have rarely achieved territorial co-extensiveness or psychological and social congruence.[34] It is salutary to recall the wave of ethnic resurgence within western Europe today, when examining the seriousness and impact of movements of ethnic secession or irredentism in contemporary Africa and Asia.[35]

Perhaps even more vital has been the sequence, and causes, of *state*-formation in western Europe, since, as we shall see, this has greatly influenced the rather different pattern of state- and nation-formation outside Europe. Looking back to the Europe of around 1500, Tilly notes some peculiar features which favoured the rise of the modern state as the dominant political unit on the continent. Among the 'pre-conditions' of state-formation, he singles out a relatively homogeneous Christian culture (with some exceptions), a largely peasant economic base with a ruling stratum of landlords rather than a tribal or lineage base, and a highly decentralised political structure, which allowed for much political conflict and therefore political takeovers. There were also some conditions which actively favoured the rise of states: first, the efficiency of the centralised state, once it was seen to work, as a political organisation superior to others; second, a special geo-political factor, namely, the freedom of much of Europe from external pressures, except in the southeast (where strong states did not have the chance to develop), a freedom that also allowed for territorial (or overseas) expansion; and finally, the growth of cities, urban trade and a merchant class, which allowed wealth to accumulate and, through taxation, helped the emerging states to finance their military and bureaucratic operations and activities.[36]

These were general factors, albeit peculiar to Europe, which favoured the rise of the 'state' form of polity as a widespread phenomenon. The routes to statehood in different parts of the continent varied greatly, and so did the factors which determined which particular candidate for statehood was likely to succeed. The different 'sequences' to statehood depended on three main types of relationship: first, the pattern of mobilisation (and in Europe, mobilisation on the basis of class, religion and language superseded all other bases); second, the extent and rate of acquiring 'stateness' in Tilly's sense; and third, the extent and manner of acquiring political rights by the governed, rights which bound the agents of the state to specific groups and concentrated those rights in the state as such, at the expense of other bodies. All these patterns and rates varied from case to case, as did the specific factors making for a successful outcome of a bid for statehood. Among the latter, Tilly includes:

1. the availability and use of extractible resources
2. a protected position — both in space and over time
3. a continuous supply of political entrepreneurs, usually kings and their ministers and generals
4. relative success in warfare with other units
5. the homogeneity of, or ability to homogenise, the territorially incorporated populations
6. the ability of the state to form strong coalitions with segments of the landed elites

Tilly thinks, on the basis of the various studies, that, with the exception of the first condition, the availability of extractible resources, success in war was probably the crucial variable in deciding whether a particular political candidate could become a viable state. For military success allowed the state to deliver resources to its populations, to mould them into a mobilised unity, to define their territories sharply, to overcome internal opposition and promote centralisation, coordination and governmental autonomy. In short, 'War made the state, and the state made war'.[37]

Finally, Tilly notes the importance of the international (or better, 'inter-state') context. Here he draws on Wallerstein's influential analysis of the growth since 1500 of a European 'world economy', around a series of core states which made all the major commercial transactions and came to dominate the 'periphery' in Latin America, Asia and even Africa (though not all strong commercial and manufacturing centres, like Holland, turned out to produce strong states).[38] But Tilly also notes the importance of the growing 'inter-state' system itself, each state in the European web coming to acknowledge the status of the others. In this context, the Treaty of Westphalia marked an important turning-point. Since that date, long wars ended by congresses and treaties have become the accepted European norm for state-creation and state-consolidation: witness the treaties of Vienna, Versailles and Yalta. Each new agreement limited the number and extent of new states which could participate in the system; and the later the period, the more did wars and ensuing treaties *create* the recent states.

From this large array of conditions and factors of European state-making, two considerations stand out. The first is that the 'Western model' is unique. That is to say, taken as a whole, it cannot illuminate the experience, social and political, of other continents, not just because the others are 'latecomers' (and hence, in these spheres as in more technical ones, can borrow directly from later stages of the process), but because some of the factors listed (for example, the geo-political and cultural ones) are peculiar to European history, and because many other areas of the world did not enjoy Europe's protected position; on the contrary, they became for a period political and economic dependencies of European states. During the period under consideration (1500 to 1900), Europe did not experience a major foreign occupation (the Ottoman threat was more or less contained); hence, like the ancient

Greek city-states, it was free to experiment and develop its special political forms without external interference. Whereas, Latin America, Asia and later Africa came more and more within the economic orbit and political domination of a militarily superior Europe.

But, as we mentioned at the outset, this very fact of colonial dependency also makes the 'Western model' a matter of crucial relevance to the African and Asian social and political experience. Or rather, the various Western models; and only some of the more general features of those models. For one result of the researches of comparative historians is to correct, and specify, the rather sweeping characterisations of European history presented by 'modernisation theories'. It is not only a matter of parochial European interest to underline the differences between, say, the Iberian, French and British historical models of state-making; or, conversely, the similar effects of rapid urbanisation and trade, and the efficiency of specialised states. Nor is the French or English or Dutch experience of homogenising diverse populations to create 'nations' irrelevant for African and Asian elites bent on forging 'nations' out of culturally heterogeneous peoples, even though social and cultural differences between the continents may make too direct a comparison misleading.

The central point, however, of the Western experience for contemporary African and Asian social and political change has been the primacy and dominance of the specialised, territorially defined and coercively monopolistic state, operating within a broader system of similar states bent on fulfilling their dual functions of internal regulation and external defence (or aggression).[39] For, although the tutelary African and Asian states differed from their European counterparts in the extent of their external sovereignty or, more usually, dependency, they too formed an integral part of the global system of states and increasingly took over the dual functions of earlier European states. In so doing, they provided the essential framework, and defined many of the tasks of the various African and Asian strata and communities, for decades to come.

2 *Imperialism and Colonialism*

Social and political change in Africa and Asia during the last two centuries has been largely intrusive in nature and exogenous in kind. Within Western Europe, social and political change can be analysed in mainly 'endogenous' terms, or at least as the product of the interplay between its constituent states and nationalities; but in Africa or even Asia since 1800, such an analysis would omit the most important types and sources of change. Not that the 'traditional societies' of Africa and Asia were stagnant, as early modernisation theory would have had us believe; there was considerable change in the 'tribal' societies of Africa and the 'oriental despotisms' of much of Asia, change that was both material — in technical innovations or new types of production — and cultural — in the spread of religions like Islam and the rise and fall of empires in both continents. Yet, from the late 18th century onwards, the course of social and political change in Africa and Asia has been increasingly conditioned by external political, cultural and economic influences stemming mainly from Europe.

It is this fact that has ensured a very considerable divergence between African and Asian patterns of change, on the one hand, and European trajectories, on the other. African and Asian patterns were bound, for this reason alone, to differ from the 'Western models' held up for emulation. The imposition of colonial regimes, direct economic exploitation of indigenous peoples and territories by Western traders and financiers, the promotion of rapid urbanisation, the slave trade, Christian missionary efforts in many lands, all attested to the power of 'intrusive' change and growing influence of exogenous sources of transformation.

Two other factors contributed to the divergence between European patterns and African and Asian experiences of social and political change. The first, obviously, stems from the quite different pre-colonial indigenous bases — social, economic and cultural — from which subsequent social change set out.[1] Where tribal and lineage corporations play such an important role in social life, as they do in many African and Asian countries, they are bound to shape the effects of imposed modern states in a manner for which Western European experience, which generally lack such corporate structures and organisations, afford no parallels and provide no models.[2] Such great differences in cultural and social organisation ensure corresponding divergences in the routes and directions of social and political change today in Europe and in Africa or Asia. Second, the difference in historical period must be borne in mind. European patterns of social and political formation established themselves in the 'early modern' period, i.e. between 1500 and 1750. They, therefore, came into being prior to, and as a model for, more recent African and Asian processes and structures. Both Europeans, and later Asian and African elites, have sought to replicate earlier European patterns, through more or less conscious and deliberate political action, by creating the new states in 'free' and 'vacant' areas. Seen in global perspective, the era of colonialism and nationalism in Africa and Asia has emerged as a 'cycle' and, to some extent, a 'product' of the expansion of the European inter-state system, after it had crystallised in the European heartlands; and, of course, that later era, the 19th and early 20th centuries, differed in vital ways from the early modern period when the European states and nations began to form.[3]

Indeed, several scholars have been struck by the peculiar features of this age of imperialism and colonialism, which so imprinted the Afro-Asian experience and differentiated it from that of its Western forbears. The fact that, during the last two decades of the 19th century, the major European powers, already engaged in fierce economic competition and soon to go to war, rushed headlong into the acquisition of vast overseas imperial territories, particularly in Africa, made a great impression on many contemporaries. So much so, that liberal and radical observers were quick to link the colonial annexations with economic developments through some overall theoretical account, the so-called 'theory of capitalist imperialism'. Of the various versions of the theory, Lenin's, for practical reasons, has become the most influential; but it, in turn, owed much to the earlier formulations by the English radical, J.A. Hobson, and the Viennese Social Democrat, Rudolf Hilferding. Hobson's theory was, admittedly, liberal and reformist. It argued that colonies were needed, as long as no social reforms were undertaken in Europe, largely because European capitalism would otherwise generate an over-supply of commodities on the domestic market and a corresponding underconsumption by the working classes. It was therefore essential to find new outlets for surplus exports, and new markets and investment opportunities, to counteract oversaving at home. For Hobson, the solution was to introduce social reforms which would give the workers greater purchasing power and better social conditions. That would regenerate metropolitan capitalism and obviate the need to annex colonies.[4]

Lenin's view was much less benign. Taking up Marx's theses that capitalism, as it evolved, tended to concentrate production and wealth, yet also show a gradual fall in the rate of profit, Lenin argued that Europe in 1916 had entered into the era of mature 'finance capital' dominated by cartels and monopolies in search of new wealth and markets, now that domestic capitalism was in a state of crisis and decay. Inevitably the cartels sought to export their surplus capital; as a result, they took on international dimensions and divided the world into competing economic spheres, to control markets and the supply of vital raw materials. This was the real meaning of modern capitalist 'imperialism'.[5] The growth of huge trusts and cartels inevitably entailed colonial annexations to ensure access to raw materials and extend their markets. In this Lenin remained true to the classic marxist account of the universality of the capitalist mode of production.[6]

Lenin owed much of his theory to the rather more sophisticated account advanced by Hilferding in 1910, which turned on the nature of 'finance capital'. Hilferding noted the way in which the great cartels utilised finance capital, the capital at the disposal of the great banks, to monopolise whole sectors of industry.[7] Tariffs were erected as weapons of trade rivalry between the cartels and the growing trend to export capital was, partly, a function of the decline of free trade, and, partly, of more favourable economic conditions overseas, including higher interest rates and cheaper labour costs. Hilferding argued that previous colonies and markets were meant to establish new consumer products, but today's colonies were different;

today new investment of capital is primarily directed towards places which deliver raw materials for industry.[8]

Hilferding saw colonies as 'places for investment', especially if they possessed mines; but the lack of a 'free' wage labour force constituted an obstacle and 'disturbance' to the advance of capitalism. To overcome it, the capitalists must appeal to 'the supreme power of the state' and its violence. Gone are the days of peaceful free trade; the new-style finance capitalism is necessarily violent, and believes in the power and greatness of the state, born of the national unification struggle, and devoted to the consolidation of imperial interests. Previous nationalism was limited; it confined itself to the boundaries of the European nation-state. Today's nationalism is, and must be, expansionist; it exalts one's own nation over all others, and aims at world supremacy for that nation, 'an ambition which is as unlimited as the struggle of capitalism for profits'. Hence the struggle for colonies;

is at root an economic phenomenon; but it is justified on ideological grounds through that peculiar transformation of the idea of the nation, which no longer recognises the right of every nation to political self-government and independence, and which no longer expresses the democratic principle of the equality of all human beings at the national level.[9]

And not only does capitalist expansion provoke imperialist nationalism; it also encourages the ideology of racism:

Thus, in the ideology of race, there develops disguised as natural science, the reality of finance capital's striving for power, which in this way can prove that its actions depend on and are made necessary by nature and science.[9]

Suggestive and plausible as Hilferding's version of the theory may be, it suffers with other variants of the idea of 'capitalist imperialism' from the basic failure to provide an adequate account of colonialism and the colonial state. At the level of theory, it remains no more than an illuminating tautology; that is to say, if we *define* 'imperialism' as overseas capital investment, then the 'theory' holds as an account of capital export, and the mechanisms it has uncovered do indeed tell us much about the workings of this stage of European capitalism. But it stops well short of explaining the need to annex colonies and the fact of overseas territorial empire. All it can do is to point to an historical correlation between the export of capital and a sudden rush to divide up 'vacant' areas of the globe, mainly in Africa, and assign them to rival European powers. To turn the theory of capital export into a full-fledged account of imperial annexation, we would have to show that European conquest overseas was actually undertaken for the purposes of capital investment and the need for markets abroad to compensate for dwindling domestic markets. To assume that each imperial annexation must serve some 'objective' capitalist 'interest' or potential (or anticipated) interest, still leaves us with the serious problem of uncovering the mechanisms of the alleged linkage between such interests and the acquisition of overseas territories.

If we examine the historical evidence for a close connection between capital export and overseas territorial annexations, the picture that emerges is a good deal more complex and variable than the theory proposes. To begin with, although there was a 'peak period' of territorial annexations in the 1880s and 1890s (notably the 'scramble for Africa'), a large part of European empire-building well antedated the stage of 'mature' finance capitalism. Leaving aside the early Portuguese and Spanish acquisition of Latin America, it could be argued that some of the most important imperial annexations occurred in the 18th century or even earlier; the examples of Australia, Canada, India, Indonesia and various Caribbean islands are only the most obvious, and they were soon followed, in the first half of the 19th century by British expansion in southern and western Africa and French annexations in North Africa.[10] Second, although the late 19th century, the period assigned by the theory to the emergence of 'finance capitalism', witnessed a rapid proliferation of colonies, by no means all European annexations can be shown to have been motivated by the need to export capital. Neither later 19th century Tsarist annexations of Central Asia and Siberia, nor pre-1914 Italian attempts to annex Abyssinia and Libya, can be put down to the needs of capital export; both countries were poor in capital and, generally, capital-borrowers for their own industrial development. Even the British annexation of Egypt after 1882 was as much political and strategic in origin; Cromer certainly encouraged capital investment in his 'modernisation' projects, but mainly as a means of strengthening British political control.[11] Third, the role assigned to financiers and industrialists by the classical marxist theory does not always square with historical facts. It is certainly true that, in the period under consideration (1870–1914), big business in Germany and Britain helped to foster a jingoistic sentiment which, in the German case, at any rate, tended to favour overseas expansion; although quite a few businessmen remained committed to the principles of free trade. On the other hand, what businessmen and industrialists wanted from overseas colonies was short-run profits or raw materials, rather than long-term investment. In a number of cases, governments had to prod their financiers and industrialists to invest in the newly conquered territories, as the French government did for its North African protectorates. Where business did export capital, it was generally to the new white dominions overseas (or to European countries): to Canada, Australia, South Africa, New Zealand, the United States and Argentina (the main exception is Malaya, of the new colonies), rather than to the 'tribal', semi-feudal or other non-capitalist economies and societies of Africa and Asia.[12] In this respect as in others, the avowed 'interests' of big business and of political leaders in the European metropolitan states were often at odds. While politicians like Ferry and Chamberlain included capital investment in their enumeration of the benefits of colonial annexations, it was mainly in order to justify on 'rational' grounds acquisitions that were being (or had been) made on a whole complex of grounds, many of them non-economic in nature. The desire for trade and for vital raw materials certainly played a part in the thinking, and even more the rationalisation, of politicians and statesmen involved in the process of overseas annexations; but so did other concerns like securing outlets for emigration, pandering to nationalistic sentiments among the 'populace', securing strategic routes and outposts like the Cape of Good Hope, attaining or maintaining status and power equivalence in the European interstate system, even the obscure passion for national *gloire*.

In sum, the classical marxist causal chain tends to oversimplify a complex situation, even for the period to which it refers (and it cannot easily cope with the subsequent 'balkanisation' of the Middle East), and it omits the role of political and prestige factors which, it can be argued, were even more central to European 'imperialism', particularly if we include earlier and later periods as well. It is true that the two facets of capitalist penetration and European interstate political rivalries can be extended backwards to the early 16th century; but, even if we accept Wallerstein's thesis, the nature and extent of capitalist penetration varied greatly as between different African and Asian territories (being rather peripheral in Africa prior to the 19th century), and it is not easy to correlate such penetration with colonial expansion either in place or time-period.[13] In some cases — the British annexations in India following the difficulties encountered by the East India Company — the causal chain seems to hold up; though even here, Anglo-French rivalries played a larger part in the actual annexations than any presumed need to satisfy the interests of City financiers and traders. In other cases, for example many of the African annexations, it is difficult to point to any marked penetration of capitalism (with some obvious exceptions) which could explain the sudden rush for 'vacant' territory. The precipitate imperial division of Africa following the Congress of Berlin, was motivated as much by status and strategic interests following the emergence of Germany and Italy as 'great powers' in the concert of European states, as by any real or alleged economic benefits accruing to big business. Ever since the 16th century, and the Treaty of Westphalia at the very latest, the idea of a European balance of power among the dynastic or oligarchic states on the continent, preoccupied the consciousness of all the upper and middle classes (and later, of the lower classes as well). The very idea of a 'great power' which came to the fore in the Baroque era, carried with it certain prestige and political implications, which easily carried over into the sphere of military expansion: and once that expansion had been halted within the narrow confines of Europe itself, once all the 'vacant' territories and excluded populations had been filled and incorporated into the new type of territorial, centralised state, overseas expansion became the likeliest prospect and the most advantageous, if great power status and power was to be enhanced. It was also a means of offsetting any temporary gains made by any one of the European great powers on the Continent itself, both in terms of strategic and territorial gains, and in the supply of raw materials (and later markets) needed to consolidate state power at home and furnish its military arsenal.[14]

I do not want to suggest that economic motives, in the broad sense, were not vitally important in the process of imperial expansion and colonial annexations. Trading missions and interests often paved the way for such annexations, even if they did not 'cause' them. But they, too, were part and parcel of the wider process of creating the European territorial state and, possibly even more crucial, of creating and maintaining the European *inter*state system. While Fieldhouse is right to point out that *particular* annexations in overseas territories had local causes, the whole process of European imperial expansion, and its central product, the colonial state, cannot be explained in purely local 'patchwork' terms. The local causes need to be fitted into a broader framework in which the perceived interests of European states, and their ruling groups, figure prominently.[15] How else can we explain why local causes so often 'suck in' European political structures as solutions and outcomes for quite different local problems? How else can we explain the massive uniformity of the 'colonial state', which, for all its local adaptations, conformed to a basic model, that of its European progenitor? For this, as we saw, was the chief legacy of European colonialism in Africa and Asia, rather than any economic system or ideology; and to the features of that colonial state I wish now to turn.

It is perhaps worth recalling that the terms 'colonialism' and 'imperialism', signified political principles and structures. Imperialism referred to the unprincipled acquisition of territory overseas, usually by force of arms, and was associated with the expansionist policies of Louis Napoleon III and of Disraeli, who quite consciously set about resuscitating or extending the French and British empires after 1850.[16] Colonialism, in turn, denoted a system of legislation in a different and politically dependent territory, with its mainly European features adapted to local conditions. It was Lenin

who, following Hobson and Hilferding, endowed these predominantly political concepts with their modern economic
content; and in doing so, Lenin bequeathed to modern scholar-
ship a specific frame of reference into which the colonial
question could be comfortably inserted. It therefore comes as
no surprise to read, in an influential modern survey of 'Third
World' problems, that

> . . . the central *raison d'etre* of imperialism is the extraction of profit from the
> labour of the indigenous people by Whites by virtue of their control over
> the political machinery of the State.[17]

For Peter Worsley, as for many others, the essence of the
colonial relationship, too, is primarily economic:

> It is no ideological assertion, but a simple generalisation rooted in empirical
> observation, that the prime content of colonial political rule was economic
> exploitation.[18]

It is true that Worsley, like others, lists several additional
features of colonial rule: the initial military takeover and paci-
fication of the area, administrative coercion exercised by
colonial officials over the colony, a racialist ideology which
served to support that coercion and explain the need for
authoritarian methods, and finally a process of psychological
exploitation or 'infantilisation', a colonisation of the personality such as was described by Mannoni in Madagascar and
Fanon in Algeria.[19] Yet, important and even indispensable as
these features of colonialism have been, they are predicated
upon the fundamental economic content and purpose behind
the whole colonial venture, which was the exploitation of
native labour and resources for the maximisation of business
profits and the solution of the crisis of domestic capitalism. In
the view of modern scholars in this Leninist tradition, colonialism operated as a single system (especially in Africa after
1885), in which missionaries, officials, businessmen and
settlers participated in varying degrees, any conflicts of
interest among them taking second place to the overriding
economic needs of that system, and of the metropolitan economic requirements it was designed to fulfil.

Recent 'dependency' theories (analysis of which lack of
space precludes) have demonstrated the undoubted benefits
derived by metropolitan powers (or at any rate their strategic

business classes) from colonial rule and its gross exploitation of the labour and resources of many dependant territories. Yet this line of argument fails to give a convincing explanation of why such exploitation took the peculiar form of the 'colonial state', even in those areas of Africa and Asia which could yield minimal economic returns for the necessary administrative and military outlay.[20] Nor can it account for the varying forms, and hence social and political effects, of the colonial state. While not denying the relevance of economic exploitation, both overt and concealed, as a crucial factor for the shape and workings of the colonial state, and indirectly therefore to its transformations by African and Asian nationalists, a more complete picture can only emerge through an examination and enumeration of the main similarities and differences in concrete colonial systems of rule.

Perhaps the main common feature of all colonial systems was the obvious, but nevertheless basic, fact of territorial definition. Territorial demarcation was, as we saw, the first of the identifying features of the modern European state; in Africa, the Middle East and south Asia, where it was an external imposition, such an exclusive emphasis upon geographical boundaries was bound to contain an element of artificiality. In the event, in Africa at any rate, the lines of demarcation were, as often as not, drawn right across pre-existing ethnic and cultural groupings, so that ethnic communities like the Ewe, Somali and Bakongo, were divided up between different colonial units, usually ruled by rival European powers.[21] As an inevitable consequence, such artificially created colonies had to rely almost exclusively upon the legitimacy of territory, and invest their boundaries with an almost sacred character, which reflected the fixities and needs of European interstate relationships. And, when it came to fostering a sense of loyalty in the culturally heterogeneous populations incorporated into a particular colonial state, it was to a sentiment of territoriality and state-wide sense of belonging that colonial rulers had to appeal, for fear of evoking alternative cultural self-definitions and allegiances.

A second unifying feature of colonial rule was its executive and bureaucratic nature. Colonialism operated essentially on the gubernatorial principle: a governor, appointed by the metropolitan political authorities, was vested with supreme powers in the colony, and represented the colony to the metropolitan territory. In this respect, despite the presence of advisory and even local consultative and legislative councils, the colonial executive branch greatly overshadowed other branches of government, acting as it did on behalf of, and often under direct orders from, the metropolitan executive arm. In an executive system, the bureaucracy inevitably becomes entrenched as the main agent of government and the chief instigator of any social change. Where there is no local parliamentary control, the administrative arm inevitably encroaches on a far wider range of issues and acquires far greater powers and scope than in contexts where its actions are subject to daily legislative scrutiny. The result is not only a stronger bureaucracy in relation to society as a whole, but also in relation to the rights and liberties of its individual members. The state is on the way to becoming stronger than society in a colonial territory, with all the consequences for subsequent social and political developments after independence that such a state of affairs entails. Despite the many differences in French, British, Belgian, Dutch and Portuguese colonial policies, the centrality and dominance of the executive arm and its bureaucratic apparatus, and the coercive monopoly that it possessed throughout the territory, constituted the fundamental constant of the colonial system and the colonial experience. In the balance of power between different colonialist interests, those of the bureaucracy itself became (if they had not originally been) the overriding determinants of social policy and social change in every European colony. Indeed, the peculiar system of rationalised administration imported from Europe, became the hallmark and essence of colonialism. It was this feature that gave colonialism such 'systemic' qualities as it possessed; bureaucracy organised and increasingly defined the character of the societies which it sought to permeate and penetrate, with varying degrees of success. It was this encounter between an alien 'rationalised' bureaucratic system and the congeries of traditional cultures and societies it sought to incorporate and mould, that determined the subsequent evolution of most African and Asian states and societies. Thus the state and its structures is not an outgrowth of society, which it then comes to dominate or rival, as in Europe; it is an alien imposition, engaged in a struggle, now latent, now overt, with the pre-colonial cultures and societies whose autochthonous roots and directions it diverts and remoulds to its own ends.[22]

Third, colonial social relationships tended to mirror this split between state and society, creating for the most part a kind of 'parallel society', in which the social structures formed by the administrative colonial apparatus were superimposed upon those of the subordinated populations.[23] The line drawn between these two societies, which often corresponded to the colour-line as well as one or more cultural differentiae, soon assumed (with some exceptions) a caste-like rigidity. Mixing between white Europeans and black Africans or brown Asians was kept to a minimum, not only through an ideology of 'race' but by an exclusive life-style based upon deliberately cultivated social and cultural conventions. While business or administrative contact between the two layers of the colonial unit was regular and frequent, social mixing was generally discouraged, even if, as in the 'bridge parties' described by E.M. Forster in India, it was thought necessary for the dominant 'caste' to meet leading and selected representatives of the subordinate society from time to time on an official basis.[24] An important function of this layering was to mask the internal differences within the ruling caste, and to lend an appearance of unity to the colonial 'system' as a whole.

That was also, in part, the function of a final common feature of colonial rule, its 'educational ideology'. It is true that some types of colonialism (notably that of Portugal in Africa) tended to favour a rather static kind of paternalist system. Most colonialisms, however, combined the latter with an ideology of 'trusteeship' and a more dynamic belief in their 'civilising mission' towards the indigenous populations. Even quite early in the 19th century, British administrators saw their task as one of educating the 'natives' for ultimate independence and self-government.[25] Of course, they combined these ideas with a firm belief in the superiority of their European culture, a necessary legitimation for the benefits derived from annexing and retaining colonies in the first place. At the same time, an educational ideology, in which the territory was seen as a trust to be developed and fitted for 'mature' self-government, could also be used to justify both the retention of the colony and, should it prove burdensome later, its eventual disposal. Hence, cultural ideologies of superiority ultimately superseded racist ones, since the latter tended to rule out all chances of indigenous 'maturation' and local development, even for African and Asian elites. That is why not all colonialisms embodied an overt racialism, even though some officials accepted crude racial notions. Too open a racist ideology would have compromised other colonial objectives; and that, even before the Western democracies were engaged in a life-and-death struggle with racial fascism in Europe itself.

Of course, there was a great deal of variation within this common structure of colonialism. Even if we leave aside the Portuguese territories, (and Portugal differed in not participating in the Second World War, as well as being ruled by a dictatorship during the mid-twentieth century), Belgian, French and British principles and practices within their African colonial possessions differed greatly. The Belgian system was largely a consequence of its peculiar origins as Leopold II's Congo Free State, created in 1885 during the period of high imperialism in Africa. When it was later (in 1908) constituted into the Belgian Congo, run from Brussels, it preserved and extended the two key features of Catholic control of education and the 'concessionary system'. The former handed over to the mainly Catholic missions all responsibility for the education of Africans up to secondary school level, and with it a vast range of welfare services; the latter handed over to the great companies (*Union Minière de Haut-Katanga, Forminière*, etc.) economic power, a legacy admittedly of Leopold's fief, but one that was incorporated as an indispensable pillar of Belgian paternalism into the colonial state itself. As a result, the Catholic Church and great companies wielded a disproportionate influence over the minds and labour of the Congolese, a fact which accounts for the high proportion of Catholics and of wage-earning urban workers compared to other African colonies. The great companies and the Church between them provided a full range of social benefits and welfare services, especially for the working-class; yet ultimate power rested with the officials in the colonial hierarchy, and was

justified in terms and theories that Thomas Hodgkin has dubbed as 'Platonism', with its 'sharp distinction, social and legal,
between Belgian philosopher-kings and the mass of African
producers'.[26] It was a system which sought to arrest, for as
long as possible, social change while allowing considerable
economic growth, and to prevent the formation of an African
political elite (despite the Congolese *évolués*) while ensuring
higher living standards and greater regimentation than in
many other African territories.[27]

French colonial policies in Africa, though generally termed
systems of 'direct rule' compared to British models, were
rather more complex, even self-contradictory. On the one
hand, they followed a belief in the essential identity between
France and its overseas possessions, first enunciated in 1792, at
the height of the Revolution. This meant that all those resident
in French colonies were, in theory, French citizens, and that
the communes of Senegal, for example, could after 1848 elect
deputies to the French National Assembly. More generally, it
entailed a policy of 'assimilation' by which Africans, after a
suitable period of Gallic education, could be turned into black
Frenchmen, even if this meant severing their cultural ties with
Africa and the mass of its population.[28] But, after French
control had been extended over large tracts of West and Equa-
torial Africa, it became impossible to maintain the theory of
identity and the practice of assimilation; and a more paternalist
system, that of the *Indigénat*, was imposed upon the mass of
uneducated Africans. The great majority of African peasants
and later workers were subjected to a special legal status, were
ruled by customary law, and liable to *travail force*; while the
administration was no longer in the hands of self-governing
urban communes, but of the French *Commandant du Cercle* or
Subdivision, a high functionary of State appointed in Paris,
until that is, the first Loi *Lamine Gueye* of 1946, which
accorded citizenship to all Africans and abolished the system of
compulsory labour.[29]

This contradictory treatment of Africans meant, not only
the often deliberate fostering of an educated African elite, but
also its identification with the colonial institutions and with
French culture, and its consequent alienation from African
culture and the African peasant masses. Gross economic and

educational inequality was tolerated, even encouraged, along with legal differences, creating thereby a dangerous gulf between elite and mass and a continuing legacy of French political and economic involvement in its former African territories even after independence, manifested in French military intervention when the integrity of 'its' ex-colonial states is threatened.

British policies of 'indirect rule' are usually contrasted with French principles, the former being described as 'pragmatic' and 'piecemeal', the latter as 'logical' or 'deductive'. In fact, British policies, though showing some internal variation, followed certain 'principles'. In West Africa, early ideas of 'trusteeship' associated with liberal theory, were gradually replaced by 'organic' conservative ideas of the role of tradition in preserving the social fabric; ideas which influenced the new British policy of ruling through the local systems of hereditary chiefs, advised by British officials and district commissioners. Inevitably, however, the administrative framework imposed by Britain eroded the power, if not the prestige, of traditional chiefs and it was only to be expected that, after the watershed of the Second World War, British policy would revert to earlier notions of trusteeship and transfer support to the newly educated elites, who had imbibed British liberal (and socialist) ideas, usually through travel and study abroad. The idea of independence, for which the British were (after 1945) openly working, was, after all, latent in the earliest liberal notions. It became therefore difficult to avoid underwriting the aims and thereby the position of these new elites, however much colonial officials might despise or insult them in day-to-day relations.[30]

The situation was rather different in East and Central Africa. Here, the mass of Africans were peasants, and even after 1945 local African bourgeoisies and proletariats were almost non-existent. Even the educated elites were tiny by comparison with their West African counterparts, and no match for the well-organised settler communities. As a result, in territories like Kenya, Tanganyika and Northern Rhodesia, nationalist movements were slow to appear, and far weaker than in colonies like the Gold Coast or Nigeria.[31] Conversely, the selfsame principle of devolution of powers from Westminster, which placed power in the hands of African elites after 1945, strengthened the hand of the settler communities. It was they who, because of their freedom of association and better early organisation, were able to take full advantage of the postWar change in British colonial policy. Settler and minority groups possessed most of the wealth and education (the criteria of the early restricted franchise) and thereby dominated a Legislative Council, organised more along the lines of estates than of modern parliamentary assemblies. So the same postWar appeal to wealth and education in place of birth as criteria of political representation and power, which boosted the position of West African elites, undermined that of their East African counterparts, wherever settler or minority interests were well established.[32]

These variations in colonial policies, along with such factors as the pace of economic development, the presence of white settlers and the special position of Christian missions, were largely responsible for the subsequent forms, scope, timing and intensity of African protest movements, culminating in territorial nationalisms. For the effects of colonial rule were as varied as the types of policy they embodied and the contradictions of principle they contained. Some colonialisms, as we saw, did their best to arrest, or contain, the forces of social change which they themselves had set in train; the best example is furnished by the contradictions of Belgian policy in the Congo. Others, like the British in Egypt or southern Nigeria, implemented fairly extensive programmes of agricultural modernisation and educational expansion. Some colonial systems encouraged a greater measure of political participation; others, like the Portuguese regimes in Angola and Mozambique, did their best to prevent such involvement. Some colonialisms encouraged thorough cultural assimilation, at least for a privileged minority, as in several French territories; others systematically discouraged such identification, on the grounds of a respect for 'native traditions', or refused to extend the level of education to encompass the full range of knowledge.

It is unhelpful, therefore, to seek to categorise such variety of principle, policy and practice within a single rubric dictated by theories of 'development' or 'underdevelopment' and treat colonial regimes as if they were 'modernisers' (even if their unintended consequences were to erode many so-called 'traditional' ties) or even to range (or rank) such regimes along a continuum of 'modernisation'.[33] Similarly, to characterise colonialism as the agent of the 'penetration of capitalism', though perhaps true in a very broad and loose sense, yields little illumination about the nature and myriad effects of colonial states, particularly outside the strictly economic sphere. As we shall see, the introduction of the capitalist mode of production varied greatly as between different parts of Africa and Asia; it cannot therefore be invoked to explain the constant elements of the colonial state or of its successor regimes.

The trouble with these blanket characterisations is not only that they fail to do justice to the variety of colonial experience, but that they detract from the considerable autonomy of the political sphere and its typical recent product, the colonial state in Africa. It is this autonomy that, for largely historical reasons, has endowed the colonial state with the specific, but simultaneously common features I have enumerated above. These features owe their nature and persistence to the peculiar circumstances of their origin: as more or less deliberate creations of European statesmen and officials, who themselves carried a general vision of their role and of the framework which lent meaning to that role. That framework was, of course, the European system of states, which had evolved from its dynastic and absolutist stage into the 19th century constitutional liberal–bureaucratic state system (although only a few European states had actually completed such an 'evolution'). It was this system, at various stages of its development, which had to be transplanted, more or less intact, into the 'vacant' territories of Africa and Asia. Hence, there was a quite conscious pursuit of the European model, or rather models, both in the realm of public life, and increasingly in private affairs as well. The resulting colonial state, as a conscious European product, was also a determined and self-conscious 'Europeaniser' in politics, culture and society. Its ruling caste aimed to mould the populations it included in its domain according to clearcut European images, modelled on the earlier policies of homogenisation carried out by absolutist monarchs and their ministers.

But, though this European origin stamped the character of the colonial state right through its period of rule, it was also a 'hybrid' type of polity; for it embodied within itself different periods of the European state-making experience and differing relationships with the pre-existing cultures, religions and societies it encountered outside Europe. It aped the constitutional European states, yet, having no democratic body at its head, harked back to earlier absolutist models. On the other hand, since the governor and his ruling caste (unlike the dynastic monarch) was responsible to overseas bodies, both parliaments and cabinets, and bound by the laws and principles they had framed, it combined elements of legal constitutionalism stemming from a later period of European state-making with a dependence uniquely its own. Ultimately responsible to a constituency over which it had no powers, it had almost as great a power over the lives of a population which did not make up its constituency as the earlier European despots had possessed over their territorial subjects. In some ways, given the advances in technology and communications, the powers of colonial governors were greater. But, on the other side, the huge cultural gulf between European rulers and African or Asian subjects, greater than anything comparable within Europe itself, placed many more obstacles in the path of homogenising and integrating the territorial populations and circumscribed considerably the effects of bureaucratic penetration and intervention into the social structures they dominated. The more cohesive and firmly underwritten by religious tradition those structures were, the greater the degree of resistance to bureaucratic engineering or regimentation (as in the Islamic societies of North Africa and the Middle East, or Hindu India); and hence the greater the 'deviation' from any straightforward European models of state formation and rationalised domination.

It may be objected that such statements of the differences between European models of political change and African or Asian developments, betray a Europocentric view of social and political change in the 'Third World'.[34] There are two answers to this charge. First, we may agree with its substance, but argue that it is in essence justified by the peculiar historical circumstances of colonial rule, which were uniquely European; and that, similarly, the European fabric and style of the resulting colonial states was an unrepeatable instance deriving from the unique fact of large-scale overseas annexations by a handful of European states within a period of two to three hundred years. To this we may add that, if we are to take the autonomy of the political sector seriously and accord it due weight in the subsequent analysis of social changes in Africa and Asia, then we must set out from a European standpoint, at least to the extent of conceding the European quality informing many of the common features of the colonial state. It was the very deliberateness with which these states were contrived and created, that helped to set them apart from the social structures which they incorporated under their jurisdictions. Hence, we cannot begin to understand the reactions to colonialism if we fail to appreciate its European character and origins.

On the other hand, such a view is clearly partial. It needs to be corrected by a closer investigation of those cultures and social structures which fell under colonial sway; and that, in turn, requires us to balance the European standpoint with an African or Asian view of colonialism. That view was provided, above all, by the nationalists who aimed to destroy the colonial system, while preserving key elements of the colonial state they inherited. Their standpoint provides us, therefore, with a valuable, if also partial, corrective; and it is to the genesis and functions of nationalism, particularly in Africa, that I now turn.

3 Nationalism in Africa

So pervasive has been the influence of the theory of 'capitalist imperialism', that to this day one of the most popular views of nationalism in the 'Third World' regards itself as a movement for national liberation and a reaction to European colonialism. Thus, Thomas Hodgkin, in his brilliant book on African nationalism, wants to use the term 'nationalism'

in a broad sense, to describe any organisation or group that explicitly asserts the rights, claims and aspirations of a given African society in opposition to European authority, whatever its institutional forms and objectives.[1]

And he goes on to include all kinds of anti-European protest movement, ranging from millennial religious cults to trades unions and party movements. In the same tradition, J.H. Kautsky defines nationalism in the 'Third World', as opposed to the linguistic nationalism of Europe itself, in terms of a country's colonial economic status:

It is opposition to colonialism so defined and to those natives who benefit from the colonial relationship that constitutes nationalism in under-developed countries.[2]

Taking an even broader canvas, Tom Nairn claims that nationalism as a whole can be regarded as a necessary product of capitalism's distorted and 'uneven' development, a conception that he owes to Ernest Gellner's analysis of the uneven spread of modernisation.[3] For Nairn, nationalism 'is forced mass-mobilisation in a position of relative helplessness (or under-development)'; and such underdevelopment is, in turn, a product of the spread of capitalism, which contains 'within itself . . . the hopeless antagonism of its own unevenness, and a consequent imperialism.'[4] This last phrase Nairn explains by showing us how capitalist development always comes to peripheral countries in the fetters of a particular metropolitan bourgeoisie, usually a West European one. The task for peri-

pheral elites and masses is to assimilate the capitalist development, while shaking themselves free of the metropolitan
fetters.

There are obvious merits to such a view of nationalism. It
undoubtedly does justice to one important aspect of the
nationalist grievance, the cry of economic exploitation which
has often accompanied European colonial annexations. It also
emphasises the exogenity of nationalism's ultimate causation,
by placing the *fons et origo* of nationalist movements ultimately
outside Africa and Asia. That is surely correct. For, while the
full development of nationalism as a political force required
hospitable local conditions, its initial impetus and *raison d'etre*
was located elsewhere − in Europe, for the most part −
although the causal chain was a complex one. Finally, the
imperialism view also relates nationalist opposition closely to
colonial status and dependant relationships.

But, exactly here, the limitations inherent in the 'anti-
colonialism' standpoint manifest themselves. For the latter can
see only the economic dependency inherent in colonialism,
and therefore cannot give due weight to those other aspects of
the colonial experience that are linked even more closely to the
rise of nationalism, above all, to the impact of territorial
division and definition, and of attempted bureaucratic homogenisation. But these are the aspects that have most clearly
determined the force and shape of nationalism in Africa and
Asia. Along with this neglect of political factors, the 'anti-
colonialism' standpoint tends to pass over in silence the
cultural features of 'ethnic' types of nationalism, including
such broader movements as pan-Africanism and pan-
Arabism. Even more important, it presents a rather partial and
'negative' view of nationalism, as a movement 'against' outside forces and enemies, but standing 'for' nothing and no-
body. But this is to miss much of the point behind a nationalist
movement: its ability to attract diverse groups, to renew itself
after attaining independence, and to provide a basis and
rationale for new social and political units and institutions. I
am not suggesting that nationalism is a morally 'positive'
force, or that it does not often display hostile and patently
destructive facets; but, to concentrate on these alone and omit
the element of social construction (whether desirable or not is

beside the point), is to court the same explanatory inadequacy as afflicts the Actonian conservative critique of nationalism.[5]

In the case of the 'anti-colonialism' standpoint, all these limitations stem from an overestimation of the links between nationalism and economic underdevelopment. Once we free ourselves from this misconception, and treat economic factors as only one set among several in the causation of nationalism, we can begin to arrive at a more comprehensive and balanced picture of the emergence of 'Third World' nationalisms in general, and African nationalisms in particular. It is to the latter that I now turn.

We may begin by dividing up, for convenience, the development of African nationalisms south of the Sahara into five phases and types. Temporally, the phases have overlapped with each other a good deal and the 'types' are really varieties of general relationships between Europeans and Africans from the mid-19th to the later 20th centuries. The five phases or types are:

1. that of 'primary resistance' movements to European incursion.
2. so-called 'millennial' protest movements against colonial rule.
3. the period of gestation, and 'adaptation', of new local strata.
4. the phase of nationalist agitation for self-rule.
5. the adoption of social programmes for the masses by nationalism.

1. *'Primary resistance'*: The term was used by J.S. Coleman to refer to various movements among Africans which opposed the gradual European penetration of the continent, and the ensuing 'scramble for Africa' in the last two decades of the 19th century.[6] Both the British and the French encountered armed opposition to their advance, especially into the interior; examples would include the Ashanti Confederation in the later Gold Coast;[7] the Zulu wars in southern Africa;[8] and the resistance of the Mossi of Upper Volta.[8] Coleman dubbed such opposition 'primary', partly because of its immediacy, an almost reflexive response to the incursions, and partly because it was basically 'traditional'. Local armies were organised to

defend an existing social system and ancient culture. The European penetration was not only political and economic, it appeared to threaten age-old ways of life and habits. Hence local chiefs marshalled their followers in a spirited defence of communal cultures and polities, organising ethnic or 'tribal' confederations like that of the Ashanti. In sum, primary resistance was mainly a dynastic, aristocratic and defensive protest against social change and it was usually put down by European force of arms, the 'tribal area' being gradually 'pacified' and reduced to a dependant status.

By no means all incursions produced this kind of resistance. Quite often, Europeans were able to incorporate areas without any organised opposition, partly because of sparse population in some parts of Africa. Where, consequently, resistance was fierce and prolonged, it was natural for subsequent nationalists to hail such movements as prototypes of their own anti-colonial efforts, and to treat their leaders as early nationalist heroes and forerunners of fully-fledged nationalist leaderships. In a sense, the later nationalists were quite justified in doing so, even if they were rather more interested in myth-making than accurate historiography. To this day, scholars are not in complete agreement about the definitional status of early resistance movements, let alone about nationalism itself. Yet, to treat these first oppositions as early instances of nationalism requires us to overlook the important differences between them and later nationalisms, differences that outweigh the similarities. For one thing, as the suffix indicates, national*ism* denotes an ideological movement and it would be straining the evidence to describe early resistance as ideologically inspired movements. For another, it ignores the great differences in the type of strata which support and lead the two kinds of 'movement', a difference which involves a whole new value and status-system. Finally, and perhaps most crucial, the key element of nationalist (as opposed to other kinds of ideological) movements is absent from early resistance movements: I mean the central concept of the 'nation' itself. For a nationalist movement, it is not the old order, or any dynastic or aristocratic segment of it, that will replace the ejected colonialists, it is the 'nation', the whole collectivity of territorially contiguous and culturally unified citizens claiming a common origin and history.[9]

2. *Millennial movements*. During the late 19th and early 20th centuries, there was a whole rash of apocalyptic and messianic movements in many parts of Africa and Asia, many of them associated with vague expectations, of a sudden and abrupt demise of the colonial order.[10] A number of self-styled prophets and messiahs emerged to preach the coming of the millennium, the end of days in which a wicked and corrupt world of sinners would be suddenly and dramatically replaced by an era of absolute justice and love, only the elect being admitted to the terrestrial New Jerusalem. As in medieval millennialisms, only true believers who waited upon the event of the divine kingdom, would reign with God and His saints on earth;[11] but, in the African case, election was reserved to Africans, since Europeans were guilty of the sins of colonialism. Messianic, often ecstatic sects formed themselves in the countryside, with congregations of Bible-singing converts, combining Christianity with African rituals and songs in syncretistic cults. It was Sundkler who distinguished these messianic or 'Zionist' sects from the more stable, and staid, 'Ethiopian' churches. More emotional and vivid in their appeal, the Zionist sects revolved around individual prophets and had a greater mass following. They were also more nativist in their ritual and liturgy, and were frequently hostile to western education and medicine — although several millennial leaders had been trained in mission schools.[12] Typical of this syndrome was the case of Kimbanguism in the Belgian Congo. Simon Kimbangu had trained as catechist and carpenter in a mission school, became a healer and prophet after receiving the call, and attracted a large following among the BaKongo in the countryside. In 1921, the Belgian authorities arrested, tried and summarily deported him; yet, even in prison and exile, his influence continued. It was hardly surprising if he saw his own role as heroic, a modern equivalent of Jesus' Passion; or that his followers should come to feel that obedience was owed to God, not the colonial Caesar.[13] Not all messianic movements turned anti-colonial; the Liberian

prophet, Wade Harris, who converted tens of thousands in the Ivory Coast during the Great War, preached submission to colonial authority.[14] Most, however, though their leaders often came from a westernised religious milieu, turned their faces against 'modernisation' and social change; the Kakists withdrew into caves for meditation, the Matswanists spoilt their ballot papers, the Kikuyu 'People of God' sect burnt all foreign utensils.[15]

How far can these 'Zionist' messianic sects be regarded as early nationalisms? In some cases, there was a clear ethnic element; Kimbanguism appealed to the BaKongo dream of restoring their ancient Kongo kingdom, identifying it with the New Jerusalem reserved for the elect. Even more important as an example of the explosive mixture of apocalyptic religion and political protest was the influence of the Watchtower movement on men like Charles Domingo and John Chilembwe, who later (in 1915) went on to lead the Nyasaland Shire Highlands Rising against British rule.[16] Yet, these were not typical. Most millennial movements, despite their anti-colonial animus, were nostalgic and backward-looking, mingling their hopes of a New Jerusalem with reverence for the cult of the ancestors, and, as we saw, opposed to most social change (even though, as a result of their mobilising un-organised peasants, their activities had unintended social consequences).[17] Besides, millennialism is by definition supernaturalist: it believes in divine intervention, not human self-help. Human activity is confined to watching and pray-ing; hope is centred on the radical abolition of a world which is hopelessly sinful, and which must be completely rejected. A pessimistic attitude of flight from the world as we know it, is not consonant with nationalist ideals for the reform and restructuring of a world which God or nature has providen-tially divided into 'nations' seeking liberation and authen-ticity.[18] Socially, too, millennial movements tend to attract quite different strata from the typical adherents of later nationalisms. They appeal particularly to the very poor and ignorant in the countryside, and geographically and occu-pationally peripheral communities — or, in a few cases, to neglected or maltreated ethnic communities, which again remain predominantly rural. They do not, on the whole, succeed in attracting adherents from the new towns, much less the new urban educated and commercial strata who form the overwhelming leadership and base for nationalist movements.

There is, however, one respect in which we can see a link, albeit an indirect one, between these early millennial movements and later nationalisms, and that is the influence of Black American ideas circulated by various religious movements like the Watchtower arm of the Jehovah Witnesses. Millennialism in Africa often acted as an unconscious conduit for the dissemination of pan-Negro ideas and a sense of African dignity and 'redemption', which fed the stream of pan-African sentiments and helped to train a new generation of African religious leaders imbued with the ideas of Black consciousness. In these respects, African millennial movements made their contribution to the growth of national feeling, even though their own intentions were far removed, and even opposed, to the ideals of nationalism.[19]

So it is, on the whole, better to treat millennialism in Africa as an expression, religious in form and content, of general discontent with European penetration, another form of 'resistance' and protest, but one that propounded no secular ideology to rectify the situation, and had no conception of the 'nation' with which it would seek to replace the present unsatisfactory state of affairs. Besides, unlike later nationalisms, millennial movements were unqualified failures, both in religious and secular terms; and we can, with few exceptions, trace no links between their failure and the later success of nationalism.

A rather more serious case as 'forerunner' of nationalism can be made out for Sundkler's 'Ethiopian' churches. These are self-governing African churches, which seceded from their European 'mother' bodies from the 1880s onwards, while retaining in their liturgy and Biblical interpretation, as well as their organisation, the European Protestant models. Again, there have been cases where secession from the parent church was mainly for ethnic reasons: a fear of the disintegrating effects of European missions was partly responsible for the formation of the Tembu church in 1884 in South Africa.[20] More often, the breakaway churches simply wanted African control over African congregations; that was the inspiration behind the first Nigerian separatist church, the United Native African Church, founded in 1891. In addition, Ethiopian churches have tended to adapt Christian ethics to African conditions, and reserve the right to interpret Scripture to the African individual. As in Europe, therefore, this 'protestant' revolt (there have been some Catholic separatist churches, too) undoubtedly directed African thoughts and sentiments to the need for African control of things African, and helped to democratise religious organisation among middle-class urban Africans. For it was in the new towns, especially, that the 'Ethiopian' churches, unlike the 'Zionist' sects, drew their following; and among more educated townsmen at that. On the other hand, it would be incorrect to categorise the separatist churches as strictly 'nationalist'. Their concern was not with the building of the 'nation' or the search for ethnic and national identity as such, but with the salvation of individual souls in an African setting by fellow-African ministers. Their contribution to the rise of African nationalisms, though important, was indirect and unintended.[21]

3. *New urban strata*. The interWar period saw a great increase in the role of new urban strata, and the beginnings of African nationalist organisations from their pre-War concern with 'native rights'.

Perhaps the most important single 'background' condition of the rise of African nationalisms was the vast expansion of older cities and the emergence of new towns, especially those amorphous concentrations found in places like Dakar, Lagos, Nairobi, Leopoldville, Abidjan, Accra and Kampala. The new towns (or the new quarters in old ones) arose partly out of the needs of European administration, but also to meet the European desire for trade. Commerce is, and has been, a *raison d'etre* of many of these towns; they are often market-places for the exchange of African primary products for European consumer goods. Commerce, too, accounted for the rapid increase in size of many of the new towns and ports, as much as fivefold in twenty or thirty years.[22] A number of factors have drawn Africans to the towns. Sometimes it is pressure of population on land resources, especially where modern methods of agriculture have not been introduced or harvests were poor or

drought occurred; sometimes it was because of commercialisation of land, as in the Gold or Ivory Coast; sometimes it was
a combination of these with the revolt of youth against the
chiefs or a failure to find the wherewithal to pay the bride-
price, or simply the employment prospects and other attractions of the city, real or imagined.[23] Whatever the reasons, and
the growth of a market (but non-industrial) economy was
vital, peasants migrated to the towns, for longer or shorter
periods, and often seasonally, to supplement their rural in-
comes, and sought employment in the growing commercial
sector and in the European administration. The better-off or
the earlier arrivals were able to form a small commercial class
of market traders and cash-crop farmers in the hinterland,
helped by the incipient penetration of capitalism in the form of
large European firms during the early 20th century in certain
parts of Africa (notably the Congo, the Rhodesian Copperbelt, Uganda and the coastal areas of Nigeria, the Gold Coast,
Ivory Coast and Sierra Leone). It is important not to exag-
gerate the role of European commercial capitalism during this
early period. It was, however, important both as a general
contributory factor in the rise of urbanisation and hence the
new movements, and more specifically in the formation of
part of the new strata.[24]

Of more immediate relevance to the formation of the new
elites who will assume the leadership of nationalist movements,
is the rapid spread of Western education in the new towns.
Education was often in the hands of mission schools, but later
the European governments themselves took a hand in the
control and expansion of secondary and higher educational
facilities. A typical example was the founding of Achimota
College in the Gold Coast in 1924, where Western subjects
were balanced by traditional African ones, providing a
popular environment for the new generation of nationalists,
among them Kwame Nkrumah.[25] French policies of assimilation, especially in Senegal, also encouraged the early growth
of an educated African elite and even the Belgians felt compelled to change their erstwhile purely 'vocational' approach
to African education and belatedly foster an *evolué* elite in the
Congo.[26] Increasing numbers of Africans had access to secondary and higher education, especially in Freetown and Lagos;

while some 4000 Africans from British territories were studying in universities and technical schools abroad in 1952, with
nearly another 1000 in African colonial universities.[27]

Western education encouraged the formation of new elites
in a number of ways. To begin with, it inculcated a sense of
exclusiveness, a feeling of being set apart from the society into
which they were born, and of being admitted into a charmed
circle on a social par with the European ruling caste. Many of
them bore English (or French) names — Bannerman, Brew,
Casely Heyford — and later began to intermarry among themselves, particularly after their conversion to Christianity.
However, these 'old' families were soon supplemented by an
influx of other educated families, and between them they
opposed the old rural chiefs and kings, and the colonial
castes.[28] Second, Western education, coupled with Christian
evangelisation, brought with it a scepticism, and sometimes
outright opposition, to traditional cults and ethnic religions.
The new skills which Western education conferred also fostered a self-reliant optimism, an ethic of self-help and a much
more rationalist type of discourse. It was not difficult in these
circumstances to come to regard tradition and ethnicity in
terms drawn from European anthropology, as so much out-
dated 'tribalism' which must be discarded if an entry was to be
effected into European civilisation and scientific culture. We
find this attempt to reconcile African values of a rather general
and vague kind with European precepts and principles, in the
earliest forerunners of Western African nationalism in the late
19th century — in Africanus Horton, Bishop Crowther and
Edward Blyden. Each of these 'proto-nationalists' accepted a
predominantly European framework of argument and discourse, but tried to insert the 'African nation' or 'Negro race'
into its scale of values and set of categories.[29] Finally, acceptance of a Western framework encouraged an internationalist
outlook, and a commitment to universal rights and concepts.
The early elites became 'assimilated'; they came close to
severing their ties with indigenous culture, which seemed
cribbed and confined by comparison with Western thought
and invention. Their travels in many lands, their wide reading
and the professional concerns that moved them as doctors,
lawyers, journalists, teachers and writers, or their trading

interests, all contributed to the broad, open and internationalist, even cosmopolitan character of the older elites.

Yet, even in these early days, a new spirit began to make
itself felt in the ranks of the urban elites. Among the lawyers
and journalists, especially, there was being voiced a growing
concern with the colonial denial of basic European freedoms
and African rights. In 1897 the Gold Coast Aborigines' Rights
Protection Society was founded to secure greater freedoms for
Africans in that territory and was later dominated by the Cape
Coast lawyer, W.E.G. Sekyi. It was followed in the 1920s by
larger, but essentially personalistic parties like Herbert
Macaulay's Nigerian National Democratic Party and Casely
Heyford's National Congress of West Africa.[30] All these
attempted to win more rights and a greater measure of social
welfare from the colonial authorities, using legal and constitutional means in the various consultative and advisory
bodies.

But success through the councils was limited. The essentially executive and bureaucratic nature of colonial regimes
soon became apparent. Indigenous elites had to appeal over the
governor's head to the metropolitan governments and parliaments, if they were to secure reforms and social change.
Particular interest therefore came to focus on opening the
ranks of the bureaucracy to men of talent, irrespective of race
or creed, for it was the upper echelons of the colonial administration, monopolised by Whites, which dominated the
governor's councils and blocked all efforts to reform. African
elites became bitterly resentful of the bureaucracy's role in
society, and of its failure to democratise its ranks and apply
universal criteria of recruitment to top posts. For, even where
colonial powers espoused a policy of 'assimilation', as in some
French territories, the number of the assimilated was held
down by various means, and a subtle, social and personal
discrimination made itself felt.[31]

We cannot say exactly how much resentment was needed to
turn educated and qualified professional Africans towards the
nationalist cause, nor mark the point at which it occurred. But
some idea of the disparity between aspirations and achieve-
ments can be gleaned from the fact that in the Gold Coast in
1949 only some 14% of the top civil service posts were held by

Africans; although by 1954 rapid progress was being made, with 38% now open to Africans. In the Western region of Nigeria, too, a large intake of Africans was delayed until 1954, with rapid Africanisation occurring thereafter. On the whole, lack of educational facilities (except in Ghana and Senegal) delayed Africanisation of the public service; but there was, additionally, an unspoken assumption that senior posts should be reserved to Europeans, that Africans were not yet 'ready' to run their own affairs. It was this assumption, and the exercise of executive power, that incensed growing numbers of the African elites who no longer accepted chiefly authority, or whose economic interests, as in the Ivory Coast, clashed with the preferential treatment accorded by the colonial rulers to European traders and farmers.[32] It was not difficult to realise that the key to power, and hence privilege, in the colonial (as later in the 'post-colonial') state, lay in unfettered mobility throughout the highly rationalised command structure of the central bureaucracy, which by-passed the usual democratic and parliamentary procedures of Western states themselves. Hence a large part of the animus of early African nationalisms was fed by this mixture of occupational and political exclusion, a feature common to many other nationalisms both in Europe and Asia.[33]

4. *The rise of nationalism.* The Second World War marked a watershed in the emergence of nationalism, and in European-African relations generally. By encouraging the military and economic participation of Africans, and African colonies, in the Allied War effort, it had profound political and psychological consequences for European colonialism and African attitudes.

The War itself, by mobilising Africans and sending them abroad, broadened their outlook and inspired them with a sense of equality with Whites, born of a common danger. It also dislocated traditional habits and routines, and provided African ex-soldiers with a stock of experiences and arguments with which to counter the usual arguments about European 'superiority'. In a War fought, in part, to combat an extreme racism with genocidal consequences, the Allies became necessarily susceptible to accusations of veiled or overt racism in the territories they controlled overseas. Besides, the need for manpower and resources from Africa, and the presence of the enemy on African soil, brought home the necessity of making political and economic concessions to those prepared to shoulder a common burden. Economically, too, the War at sea disrupted the pattern of colonial exports and trade. The inhabitants of African territories soon came to feel the effects, albeit less acutely than some of the European countries themselves, as the second European War became the first real World War.[34] The effects for Africans themselves tended to be felt on a territory-wide scale, being transmitted colony by colony and refracted through the prism of administrative regulations enforced throughout a given territory. Hence, the War greatly enhanced the sense of 'territoriality' and territorial bonds among the populations in each colony, a sense that colonial governments had been seeking to instil even where 'indirect rule' was practised.

The growing sense of a territorial political community among the populations of West Africa, in particular, soon found expression in the creation of large-scale party organisations in the immediate aftermath of the end of the Second World War. Indeed, given the solvent effects of that war, it came as no great surprise that the incipient pre-War nationalism of the tiny elites should suddenly erupt in full-scale nationalist movements bent on immediate transfer of power, or at least 'home rule' for each territory. The parties founded by the new generation of leaders, recently returned from America and Europe, men like Azikiwe, Nkrumah and Kenyatta, were more radical and appealed to ex-servicemen who could not find jobs worthy of their experience, as well as the newly educated young men. They also drew on the various urban associations, some of them general improvement societies, others welfare unions, and still others ethnic or 'tribal' associations.[35] At this early stage, even the ethnic unions provided a springboard for a wider, state-wide nationalism, or appeared to combine ethnic with territorial concerns. Only later did the difference become politically relevant.

What was the nature and content of this new broader nationalism? African nationalism of the 1945-60 period, the era of independence, had three main characteristics: territorialism, democracy and pan–Africanism. Perhaps the most durable and far-reaching of these features was the 'territorial' nature of most African nationalisms south of the Sahara. This was, in large part, a function of the success of the colonial state in imprinting itself on the popular consciousness, and hence of its capacity for homogenising diverse peoples into a single political community. The European state-makers were highly successful in imposing the territorial aspect of the Western state on the African demographic and political map, and hence they were able to draw sharp boundaries, not only in political and economic reality, but also in the psychic identity and cultural vision of the new elites. The state as the basis of extraction, centralised authority, autonomous institutions and monopolistic coercion was a boundary-defining unit, a body with a distinct territorial focus and jurisdiction; its 'face' and 'shape' were largely determined by the fact and shape of the territory it controlled. Hence, the nature of the state spilt over into the definition of the nationalism that arose to challenge the rulers of the state. It was not the state *per se* that was challenged, much less its rights over a recognised territory and demarcated populations (despite some boundary disputes early on): it was merely the right of those who controlled that territorial state that was in question.[36]

There were other reasons for the 'territorial' nature and inspiration of postWar nationalisms in Africa. Colonial administrations were much more centralised than anything Africa had known before. They were centred on a capital city, exchanged goods in a unified economic market system, promulgated state-wide laws and regulations, and taxed and conscripted the subject populations across the whole territory. It was hardly surprising, therefore, if the nationalist response to this centralised bureaucratic intervention should not also assume a territorial form commensurate with that of its opponent; or that African nationalisms should organise themselves in centralised parties, based upon the capital, and exhibiting a low level of tolerance for locally based, regional or ethnic parties and movements, which might pre-empt grass roots support from the radical territorial parties. *Per contra*, the central parties like Nkrumah's Convention People's Party in the Gold Coast, sought to outbid local movements by opening local branches in the rural districts and small towns. Similarly, African nationalisms were following the example of the colonial state in its coercive monopoly. They too claimed the legitimate monopoly of force, or the threat thereof, within a given territory, they too came increasingly to rely on executive methods, particularly in those cases where opposition to their claims by the colonial power forced them into mobilising and incorporating large numbers of people in a show of strength. The Party became a 'counter-state', a sort of state in embryo, ready to take over the colonial apparatus once independence was achieved; like the colonial state, it too could tolerate no rival power centre within its territorial domain. All these facets of territorialism, coupled with the high degree of autonomy and visibility of the colonial bureaucratic apparatus, made it an obvious framework for African nationalisms, just as the state itself became its obvious target. A good part of early African nationalisms could be explained in terms of protest against the bureaucratic state of the colonial powers, in the name of those very ideals propounded by colonialists at home, and with the object of making that state accountable and later transferring it to the populations on whose behalf it ostensibly existed.[37]

If African nationalism aimed to take over the territorial-bureaucratic State which it inherited from the colonial powers, if its character was consequently largely shaped by *étatiste* presuppositions and State institutions, it also sought to utilise its legacy for its own purposes and harness it for its ideological ends. Those ends were based, in turn, on two traditions and sets of conceptions: an adaptation of the European democratic ideals, and the culture of panAfricanism. PostWar African nationalisms drew mainly on English and French democratic nationalist conceptions, particularly Mill, Rousseau and Michelet. German and Italian 'romantic' nationalisms with their emphasis on culture and language, from Herder to Mazzini, had little impact on the African consciousness, except in marginal instances.[38] It was the more 'voluntarist' political nationalisms of French and English thinkers that found favour and inspired the goals and programmes of African nationalist elites: their libertarian, egalitarian and communitarian ideals were amply reflected in the aims and content of African 'territorial' nationalisms.[39]

To grasp the democratic impetus of African 'territorial' nationalisms, we need only recall the fragile elitist social base of most African movements. To begin with, there were few African 'nations', and very few that corresponded, even approximately, with the borders of ex-colonial states. Some of the larger, or more distinctive and self-conscious, ethnic communities were already 'nations', or were well on the way to achieving that coveted status. Others were hardly more than 'ethnic categories' and between these two poles lay a host of ill-defined and barely self-conscious or politicised, local ethnic communities, many of them small and scattered. In these circumstances, African nationalists felt they had to 'construct' the nation; they had to extract it from the husk of the bureaucratic-territorial states they inherited. In Robert Rotberg's term, theirs were 'nations of intent'.[40] The new nation would take shape on the basis of a 'political community' rather than an ethnic community. Like Switzerland, they would pool their different African cultures, and from that amalgam and the common colonial and bureaucratic heritage, they would form distinctive Ghanaian, Nigerian, Senegalese or Tanzanian 'nations'. As in Switzerland, the process of assimilation and coalescence would take time, though preferably decades rather than centuries, but the result would be as thorough in its cultural uniqueness and identity, and its sense of historical patriotism, as the Swiss experience had been.[41] To fail in this endeavour, to fall short of that common identity and sense of historic patriotism, would mean an inevitable fragmentation and dissolution, such as had plagued the Balkan states in the last two centuries.

In the second place, to bind everyone equally into a political community, African nationalists, themselves often a tiny elite, had to base their appeal on the principle of popular sovereignty and the widest possible franchise. Hence, they naturally appealed to the principles of 1793, in the French territories, and the arguments of Mill and the 1867 Reform bill, in the British territories. Theirs became, perforce, an essentially 'demotic' nationalism, aiming to reintegrate the leaderships with the masses, the western-educated urban elites and the vast reservoirs of the African peasantry with their 'folk' cultures. It was no accident, too, that African nationalist movements, once they were able to organise themselves and operate fairly freely, began to adopt Western-style parties and broad congresses, often under the direct inspiration of metropolitan parties; and that they sometimes aimed to extend their appeal into the countryside through local Party branches, like Nkrumah's Convention People's Party in the early 1950s.[42] In rhetoric, if by no means always in practice, radical African nationalism became 'mass-mobilising', attempting to incorporate the majority of the population at least symbolically, even where the movement was chary of involving workers' or peasants' organisations. Such rhetoric should not be simply interpreted as a counterweight to the slights of colonial governors, who often remarked upon the unrepresentativeness and exclusive character of African elites: it is part and parcel of the very concept of a 'territorial nation' in the African context. Even if African nationalists did not often actually 'invite the masses' into history, as Tom Nairn asserts of the nationalist intelligentsia generally, they did so symbolically and in theory, as a consequence and inevitable correlative of their idea of an African 'nation', and not simply to manipulate them or utilise their numbers against the colonial master.[43]

And finally, the democratic nature of African nationalism derived its force from the interplay of colonial State and nationalist movement, whose expression was the various Party and extra-Party institutions – educational, financial, voluntary associations, trades union – which grew up in opposition to the colonial State, but had to be grafted on to that State, when it was taken over by the nationalists on independence. For, on the one hand, African nationalisms wanted to take over intact the colonial apparatus of power and order, and set it to work for the 'nation-to-be', while Africanising its personnel as quickly as practicable. On the other hand, they had to 'surround' and direct the bureaucratic apparatus through the embryo 'counter-state' of the Party and extra-Party organisations, which themselves constituted a sort of infrastructure of the nation-to-be and which alone could incorporate and mobilise large numbers of people for popular participation. That is why the very concept of 'nation-building' fits so well the activities of African nationalists as they themselves liked to see their own activities; if the 'nation' had to be created, or was in some sense 'deficient', it was imperative to 'build' it or repair it by a judicious combination of State and Party organs, able to harmonise mobilisation with social control. So a democratic 'one man–one vote' appeal is built into the very fabric of the situation in which African nationalisms have had to operate, and in particular the dialectic of ex-colonial State and aspiring nationalist movement and Party.[44]

Although territorialism and democratic ideals account for a good deal of the content and nature of African nationalisms, they only make sense within a broader context of panAfrican culture. That culture was vital for a number of reasons. In the first place, the cry that 'We are all Africans now' was an indispensable means of self-differentation from white Eruo-pean overlords and of building constructively on the bitter common legacy and experience of colonialism.[45] The appeal to colour-consciousness aided the sense of separateness and dis-tance, and threw Africans back on each other for succour and comfort. Second, by utilising race-consciousness for unifying ends, it was hoped to counteract the incipient ethnic separat-ism, and the even greater risk and fear of such movements. 'Pan-Africanism' being as indigenous as 'tribalism', could be used to counter the latter's influence and bolster the 'artificial' content of territorial nationalisms. People might cast doubts on the validity of Nigerian as opposed to Ibo and Yoruba, or Kenyan as opposed to Kikuyu or Luo, culture and identity; but there could be no such doubts with a panAfrican identity and culture. By showing that Nigerian or Kenyan nationalisms were 'authentically' African, any nagging sense of their alien nature could be dispelled. Third, panAfrican culture, wider than the simple movement for continental or sub-Saharan unification, helped to link up the nationalist leaders in several African territories with their West Indian and American Black counterparts. Thus, the fifth panAfrican Congress in Man-chester brought together, among others, du Bois, George Padmore, Nkrumah and Kenyatta; and Legum has shown through a variety of documents and poems how panAfrican culture has cross-fertilised different continents and provided a common framework of discourse for Blacks all over the world.[46] And, finally, at the most general and deepest levels, panAfrican culture has greatly facilitated the quest for moral regeneration and rediscovery of an innate Black dignity, which was felt to have been lost and tarnished by the humiliations of slavery and colonialism. By spurring the efforts at historical rediscovery of the African pre-colonial heritage by African scholars like Cheikh Anta Diop, panAfricanism contributed to that extension of the African identity in time, which is so vital to the recovery of dignity and self-confidence.[47] 'No roots, no dignity': panAfricanism, through its historical investigations and its poetic evocations of an African personality and community, at once spiritual and natural, the antithesis of Western materialism and corruption and technical aridity, has fed the quest for Négritude in which all that is black is felt to be noble and beautiful, and has helped African intelligentsia to find solace from the 'white man's menace, out of time', and a revived sense of their place in the global scheme, an honoured if special status, different but no longer outcast and alien.[48]

In many ways, it is the panAfrican culture that gives African nationalisms their distinctive, indeed unique, flavour. Though its themes may be paralleled in many other nationalist ideologies all over the world, their combination and intensity is matched perhaps only by the Zionist movement to which they so often likened themselves.[49] And yet, taken all in all, the truth about much African nationalism is more prosaic: they are first and foremost 'territorial' nationalisms, lacking the poetry and florid fancy of many an East European nationalism, but also, partly for that very reason, more firmly grounded in the Western tradition of democratic sovereignty and national egalitarianism.

But, however we view the nature and content of African nationalisms, three things are clear, and they go far towards correcting the bias of both the 'anti-colonial' and 'uneven development' theses on nationalism, as it manifested itself south of the Sahara, at any rate. First, and most obviously, African nationalism from its inception had clear 'positive' programmes and ideals, which went beyond a simple opposition to colonial European authority, or to imperialism or capitalist (or any other) exploitation. Their aim, then and always, has been the same as that of nationalists everywhere: to set up 'nations', autonomous, unified and with a clear cultural identity, but on the pre-existing basis of the territorial 'grid' of states imposed on Africa by the colonial powers (and for this reason, we reserve the term 'nationalism' for the post-1918 movements and exclude simple opposition which sought a return to the *status quo ante*, rather than a new 'national' order).

Second, and arising out of this historical peculiarity, African nationalisms formed themselves on the basis and within the framework of the very territorial and bureaucratic state they so deplored. It was this colonial state that became the mould as well as the target of African nationalisms, and on them it stamped its special character and aims. Hence, it is not so much imperialist (or indigenous) capitalism that has shaped the aims and character of African nationalism; rather, it has been the special features of the colonial state — gubernatorial, terri-torial, bureaucratic, paternalist-educational, caste-like — that have given them its peculiar impetus and shape. Colonial policies, notably in the educational sphere, have been vital in both creating new strata and turning them into anti-traditional elites; and with Christianity, they have been major factors, both directly and indirectly, in creating the content and goals of African nationalisms.[50]

Finally, it becomes more difficult to view African nationa-lisms and the rise of African states as a direct or even indirect product of capitalist penetration. The emergence of African states in the 1950s and 1960s was largely a consequence of geo-political changes, notably the demise of European colonialism, itself a result of the decline of Europe after two costly Wars and the rise of America and Russia, neither of which had colonies in Africa. It was also an effect of the negative attitude of the two superpowers towards colonial empires; and even more, of the hold on the minds of all parties of the Western conception of the State and the need, equally felt on all sides, to fill any power vacuum created by declining colonialism, notably after the various wars and ensuing treaties which proclaimed the right of national self-deter-mination.

The rise and nature of African nationalisms is rather more

complicated. There is no doubt that, from 1918 onwards (in a very few cases, even earlier), capitalist exchange began to make inroads into the African interior — till then it had largely confined itself to coastal areas in West and East Africa. Commerce was of undoubted importance in fostering a small, but active, native bourgeoisie engaged in long-distance trade for the most part, rather than in setting up factories for the production of local goods (an exception was the field of mining, though here finance, know-how and technology were mainly European). Indirectly, commercial exchange and cash crop production, where it occurred, encouraged more open attitudes and greater urbanisation; and these, in turn, aided the efforts of missions and governments to foster western education. Nevertheless, an African bourgeoisie of any size and force was generally lacking until the 1960s; and likewise, a proletariat was (and often remains) minimal. Capitalist production, as opposed to capitalist exchange, was confined to certain areas before the 1960s, and they constituted small enclaves in the vast landmass of Africa.[51] Hence, given the paucity of capitalist penetration and the late entry of capitalist *production* (as opposed to exchange relations), we can hardly read off the rise and shape of African nationalisms from the 'uneven development' of capitalism in Africa. The business history of Africa certainly forms an important chapter of its relations with Europe and its overall development; but it was neither large nor significant early enough to account for the genesis and nature of African nationalisms.[52]

African nationalisms have sprung up in the most unlikely places, if we accept the 'uneven development' thesis, or indeed any theory that would link nationalism too closely with economic development. By no stretch of the imagination could we class either Somalia or Eritrea as being among the more economically developed, or capitalistically 'penetrated', areas of sub-Saharan Africa; yet it is just in these two ethnic areas that we find the fiercest contemporary expression of nationalism. In the early 1950s, Kenya and Togoland were not among the most developed areas, even though more advanced then than Somalia is today; yet, just here, among Kikuyu and Ewe, there erupted two of the most active, even violent, of nationalisms. In Mali, one of the poorest states of Africa, the nationalist movement proved to be one of the most radical and activist, as did the Tanganyikan movement in a state which was not nearly as advanced as its East African neighbours.[53] In other words, the intensity and origins of a given nationalism are more the product of the political and cultural factors at work within a particular territory as well as more generally, rather than of the degree to which the capitalist mode of production has begun to penetrate the social structure. While it is true, that at the most general level, commercial exchange nearly everywhere antedated, in some degree, the emergence of nationalism in Africa, so did a host of other factors, all of which can be shown to have contributed in some measure to its rise. There is no means of knowing how much capitalist penetration is necessary to stir a people or territory into nationalist activity; and there is no real reason to single out capitalist penetration or uneven development for special causal treatment. It is rather to the strength of bureaucratic control and territorial definition, as well as educational impact, that we need to look; for the origins and force of given nationalisms tend to correlate far more closely with these factors, and the colonial policies that stemmed from them, than with any input of capitalist exchange or production.

4 Ethnicity and Class

During the 1960s, the first decade of African independence, African and Asian leaders commonly dwelt on the gulf that separated their societies from those of the West. The West, it was suggested, was not only materialistic and corrupt; its societies were deeply divided and torn by ethnic, class and sectarian conflict. Western society was mechanical, 'atomistic' and therefore soulless, while the societies of Africa and Asia were harmonious, 'natural' and 'organic'. Society in the West was built up piecemeal around the individual and his desires; African and Asian societies were genuine communities of which the individuals were integral parts, their significance and purpose deriving solely from participation in the whole.[1] African and Asian leaders, and their Western apologists, like the 19th century Russian Slavophiles before them, felt that their own societies embodied the 'communitarian' ideal preached by Rousseau and delineated by Tönnies and Durkheim, but in practice so sadly absent in the West itself.[2] It was because of their community spirit that African and Asian societies were relatively free of those sectional cleavages and conflicts which had been Europe's undoing and which now threatened to tear America apart.[3] Such conflicts as were to be found in nonWestern societies, were either the exaggerated inventions of foreign intellectuals, or foreign and quite minor importations. African and Asian societies were basically classless and nationally integrated; they had no room for the sort of alienation and conflict endemic in the West.[4]

But, as the decade wore on and multiparty states gave way to single-party rule or military dictatorships, as the newly independent states failed to disentangle themselves from the grip of capitalism and 'neo-colonialism' and thus achieve their development goals, so the issue of internal divisions within African and Asian states came more and more to the fore. One could, of course, lay much of the blame for developmental failures or lack of effective government on the pressures of the multi-nationals and the client status of many new states; but it was much harder to blame colonialism for the continuing and growing manifestations of ethnic divisions and antagonisms, or for the rise of mass politics based on the growing power of trades union. Ethnic and class conflict, in particular, possessed an independent force and constancy that appeared to presage the shape of things to come, irrespective of their colonial roots. It is therefore necessary to enquire more closely into the role of ethnicity and class, especially in Africa.

To African leaders, the term 'tribalism' conjures up an image of the evil effects of the colonial heritage which they seek to avoid. It is a term fraught with emotion, evoking the Balkan model of ethnic fragmentation and consequent dependence upon external forces and powers, which ultimately embroiled the great powers in global war. Political and economic depen-dance through such 'balkanisation', an image taken directly from southern European examples, is the greatest fear of African (and to a lesser extent, Asian) leaderships.[5] For, they argue, only through 'balkanisation' which continues the colonial policy of 'divide and rule', can the West (or other great powers) achieve their political and economic goals in Africa, which, in a nutshell, constitute the ends of 'neo-colonialism'; and only, conversely, in unity and territorial integrity, can African states escape the neo-colonial net and achieve parity of status with their European mentors.[6]

The Trojan horse of balkanisation is 'tribalism'. Few African, and not many Asian, states are free of internal cultural divisions with which they must wrestle and whose consti-tuents they must placate in matters of employment and the distribution of goods and services, if they are to head off ethnic discontent and even threats of secession. Disparage 'tribalism' as they may, the leaders of the new states must often make a series of concessions along ethnic lines, amounting to an open policy of 'ethnic arithmetic', the distribution of posts and services in proportion to the numbers of the main ethnic communities in a state, and so install and institutionalise ethnicity as the main principle of communal classification.[7] The more they do so, the more they undermine the integrity and cohesion of the often fragile new states, and the more the principle of territorial loyalty and citizenship is supplemented or replaced by that of ethnic loyalty and community. In Africa and Asia, that often appears to mean, in practice, recognising the potency and political relevance of the 'tribe' as the key internal subdivision.

Actually, the definition of the term 'tribe' is fraught with misunderstanding and confusion. It is necessary, in the first place, to distinguish the 'tribal' phenomenon in the country-side prior to urbanisation and independence, and the classification by ethnicity in the towns, especially after independence, and its attendant image of 'tribalism'. In the rural areas, anthropologists have often adopted conflicting usages of the term 'tribe'. When they speak of 'acephalous tribes' like the Nuer, writers like Evans-Pritchard and Wagner waver between a 'political' and a 'kinship' usage of the term; in the latter the tribe is a unit based upon ties of kinship and consists in a loose organisation of segments — families, clans and lineages — which share common rites and myths of ancestry, and occupy a given local area.[8] Others take the term to cover what we roughly mean by a 'people', a group with a common culture and sense of ancestry, and often a common language. Thus Vansina defines the tribe as a

community which believes that it is culturally different from all other communities around it, a belief shared by the surrounding communities.[9]

Murdock's peoples, too, turn out to be tribes, since his Index of Tribal Names is really a list of every kind of African people, who are all by implication tribesmen.[10] Still others prefer a political to a cultural definition of the tribe: tribes are territorial groups with a public organisation, they constitute political corporations with segmentary subdivisions, and are organised for dispute settlement and warfare with other tribes. This is the usage preferred by Lucy Mair; it is also the sense of Audrey Richards' analysis of the Bemba in Zambia, though she also calls the Bemba a 'nation'.[11] And the idea that tribes form to settle disputes (and for warfare) informs Middleton's description of the Lugbara in central Africa.[12]

In all these cases, however, anthropologists tend to regard the rural 'tribe' as a working social system well adjusted to meet the ecological, economic and social conditions of its environment, and as a kinship-based system which may (or may not) produce a clear political organisation, but which carries with it a definite set of role relationships and statuses.[13]

By contrast, sociological analyses of 'tribes' and 'tribalism' in the new towns tend to focus on its classificatory role, cultural or political or both, and to underplay its kinship elements. In fact, definitions tend to be functional; they designate the functions of tribalism as a means of classifying migrants to the new towns, or to new quarters of old towns. In this sense, the 'tribe' is seen less as force for tradition and conservatism, than as a means of grouping Africans of diverse origins and providing them with a variety of welfare services. The tribe becomes a basis for group identity and hence for cleavages in the city, and it also provides a resolution for problems of personal identity, for those who have been recently uprooted from their habitual way of life.[14] Finally, through its mobilisation of support, it comes to act as a channel for political aspirations, so that politics in Africa and parts of Asia — in Malaysia, Burma, Indonesia, India, Ceylon and Pakistan, as in Iraq and Iran — becomes increasingly communal and ethnic in kind.

Before we can go on to consider the role of 'tribalism' and ethnicity as divisive (or otherwise) factors in the new states, we have to steer a course through the terminological confusions surrounding the various usages of 'tribe' and 'tribalism'. The terms themselves are of European origin, and reflect, not merely confusion over the sheer variety and number of ethnic and political groupings in pre-colonial African (and to a lesser extent, Asian) societies, but also the assumption that

African societies, as distinct from others perhaps of a Western type, can be aptly described as 'tribal', in the sense that they all share some basic feature, even though this feature is neither consistently adduced nor consistently demonstrated.[15]

Once again, evolutionist assumptions are integrally bound up with Western ethnocentrism; the notion of a determinate and universal trend from simple to complex forms, through which all areas will gradually evolve, places African and even Asian experience towards the chronologically earlier and logically simpler pole of the continuum. The result is that two kinds of grouping, the 'tribe' proper and the 'ethnic community', are lumped together under the pejorative rubric of 'tribalism', irrespective of size of the community or criterion of its classi-fication. Of course, in field experience, the referents of the two concepts will overlap, as for that matter will the referents of the two concepts, 'ethnic community' and 'nation'; but that is not a good reason for not insisting on their analytic distinction.

It seems better, therefore, to reserve the term 'tribe' for a rather small group differentiated by a separate system of kin-ship relations, composed of clans who claim a common ancestor, thereby constituting a political division of any larger cultural group, like the twelve tribes of ancient Israel.[16] A 'tribe' can then be distinguished from an 'ethnic community'; the latter denotes a social group whose basis of differentiation is a common sense of ancestry and origins, the possession of a common history, and the sharing of one or more cultural traits by all its members, be this religion, mores or language.[17] Generally speaking, ethnic communities are far too large to possess any kinship basis; their sense of common descent is only a myth, albeit a powerful one. Moreover, an ethnic community, though it must claim to hail from a given locality or land, need no longer be in possession of that territory; it may have migrated, as did the Seljuk and Ottoman Turks, or be scattered across the earth, as with Armenians, Gypsies and Jews. If, however, it wants to exert political pressure, the possession of a given locality or territory, or a link of solidarity with it, is a vital instrument for achieving its goals.

Both the smaller, kinship-based 'tribes' and the historic culture-community, or ethnic community, must in turn be distinguished from the 'nation'. For, although it shares with the ethnic community a cultural basis and common way of life, a 'nation' proper is a more abstract ideal, a construct of nationalists; and hence its delineation is more difficult. To begin with, a real 'nation' must actually be in possession of its 'homeland', its territory, or acquire one that is recognisably the same. Second, the nation must manifest a single occupa-tional hierarchy, a unified system of the division of labour, which assures unimpeded geographical and social mobility. And third, the nation is a political organisation that, in theory, at least, assures to its members equal rights of citizenship and equal obligations to the collectivity. For these reasons, we find that 'nations' typically tend to aspire to statehood, or at any rate 'home rule' within a more federal structure; in Max Weber's words,

a nation is a community of sentiment which would adequately manifest itself in a state of its own; hence, a nation is a community which normally tends to produce a state of its own.[18]

Hence, in addition to features drawn from the 'ethnic community', the concept of the 'nation' adds territorial, economic and above all political elements to fashion an often ambiguous, but nonetheless emotionally solidary, composite unity, in whose name constant demands are voiced for both internal and external change and reform.[19] The demands of nationalism, which go far beyond a simple ejection of 'the foreigner' and 'the colonialist' blend into an ideological movement for attaining and maintaining autonomy, unity and identity of a social group, some of whose members conceive it to be an actual or potential 'nation'.[20]

In Africa, today, we find examples of all three groupings to which the concepts of 'tribe', 'ethnic community' and 'nation' may be usefully applied. With cases like the Tallensi or Lugusi (in Kenya), we may legitimately speak of 'tribes'; whereas the Luo, Wolof and Lulua constitute 'ethnic communities', and the Ibo, Somali and BaKongo are well on the way to becoming 'nations' (as an ideal-typical construct, it is never quite clear whether and when a given case may be said to have attained to that status). To call all these 'tribes' and their common sentiment 'tribalism', can only breed confusion and mislead politically.

In fact, in many ways the term 'tribalism' is a misnomer. For it is not advanced to describe a pre-existing rural state, but the far more recently developed urban system of ethnic classification. So-called 'detribalisation' of rural immigrants to the towns has allowed for a new 're-classification' in the city, a classification by local origin and culture. Hence, it is misleading to speak of urban 're-tribalisation' as if it entailed some kind of return to the *status quo ante*. The urban re-classification is new in its meanings and effects, even if it utilises pre-existing rural names. Thus Abner Cohen comments on the long process of Hausa migration to Yoruba towns in southern

Nigeria as one of 're-tribalisation', but argues that the tribalism of the modern urban quarters is more political than
cultural in nature and 'is not . . . an archaic survival arrange-
ment carried over into the present by conservative people'.[21] A
man's Hausa identity, he argues, expresses his relationships
with the urban social system and the interests that arise from it;
he does not eat and dress differently, speak a different language
and intermarry with Hausa because of nostalgia for the past, or
traditional conservatism, but for current social and political
purposes such as control of the long-distance cattle trade. It is
not for the sake of family ties or to retain rural role relations
and traditions that they emphasise their cultural uniqueness;
rather they use family networks and rural ties to create a
modern, but exclusive urban culture, which will give them a
political base for urban competition. In the town, then, we
should rather speak of a growing 'ethnicism', for the rural and
traditional 'tribal' grouping has given way to a relatively new
formation, the urban 'ethnic community' which seeks propor-
tionate political power and forms urban political organisations.

With these conceptual distinctions in mind, we may now
return to our discussion of the divisive role of ethnicity in the
new states, especially in Africa. What we increasingly find
today is that the earlier type of 'territorial' nationalism which
sought and won independence in Africa and Asia, is coming
under increasing attack from a more recent 'ethnic' type of
nationalism within and even across existing territorial boundaries. These new nationalisms find their base in politicised
ethnic communities and are propagated by the urban intelligentsia of those communities. Thus in Ethiopia today, a
marxist regime attempts to preserve the inherited territorial
domain of Ethiopia's former empire, while its severest challenges come from politicised ethnic communities like the
Galla, Tigre and Eritreans, some of whom actually want to
secede and set up their own independent states.[22] Neighbour-
ing Somalia is itself actuated by a fervent Somali irredentist
ethnic nationalism which seeks the return of co-ethnics and
their territories to an enlarged Somali nation-state.[23] In Kenya
and Uganda, Kikuyu, Luo, Ganda and other large ethnic
communities compete for influence and power.[24] In the

former Belgian Congo, there have been several episodes of ethnic conflict and even attempted secession, as among the Lunda in Katanga.[25] Civil war in Angola is based upon ethnic cleavages between the Ovimbundu, the Akwambundu and the BaKongo, who straddle the Congolese border.[26] Ethnic divisions have also helped to bring down the marxist government of Cabral in Guinea-Bissau;[27] while ethnic and regional conflict racked Nigeria in the 1960s, leading to the breakaway state of Biafra and ensuing civil war.[28] In Ghana, Sierra Leone, Senegal and Upper Volta, major ethnic communities have emerged as political forces, and in a few cases have sought greater autonomy, or, as in the struggle for Zimbabwe, fielded rival guerilla armies. Very few African states have been spared ethnic conflict or competition; and, if we recall the demands and activities of such disparate communities as the Kabyles, Copts, Palestinians, Kurds, Turkmen, Pathan, Baluchis, Nagas, Mizos, Shan, Karen, Malaysian Chinese, Tamils, South Moluccans, Moros and Tibetans, not many Asian states have escaped the centrifugal forces of ethnic protest and separatism. And, even if few ethnic communities have aimed for full independence, and even fewer have succeeded, ethnic cleavage has been fundamental to most African and Asian states, and ethnic conflict has been endemic.[31]

How shall we then describe these conflicts? Should they be designated 'ethnic nationalisms'? Or merely cultural 'subnationalisms', and the communities they subserve 'subnations'? That is the way several Africanists see them;[30] and more than one scholar has found a parallel in Europe's 'subnations', its ethnic minority communities within the plural states of Western Europe — communities like the Basques, Bretons, Scots and Flemish.[31]

More than terminology is at stake here, for the adoption of terms like 'subnation' (like that of tribe) indicates a political or ideological preference, in this case for the preservation of the political *status quo*, based upon existing state boundaries. But, is there such a difference between the ethnic status of, say, the Bretons and the French, or the Scots and the English, such that the first community of each pair must be accorded a lower ethnic status, and be treated as a subvariety of the second? Can we reasonably affirm a qualitative difference between the aims and aspirations of the BaKongo, Ashanti, Eritreans and Kurds, on the one hand, and the Congolese, Ghanaians, Ethiopians and Iraquis, on the other hand, such that the first set must be termed 'subnationalisms' and the second fully-fledged 'nationalisms'? That seems to be the position adopted, in their different ways, by scholars like Geertz and Silvert; but it does scant justice to the status of the claims of 'ethnic' nationalisms, while accepting the validity and importance of those of 'territorial' or state-based nationalisms.[32] We seem to be making assertions involving value-judgements about the relative status of various social and political groupings, on the basis of their alleged 'viability' as potential 'nations'. In this often tacit argument, size and scale are often taken as the key factors in determining the status of nationhood being conferred on a given community or potential community; a 'nation' allegedly must be 'large', large enough for 'survival' in the modern world.[33]

I do not want to assert that size and scale are irrelevant to the growth of 'nations', and do not enter at some level into the determination of these units of population. Unfortunately, both criteria are extremely variable; on the one hand, we have the Russian or German nations with tens of millions of members and occupying huge areas, and on the other small island communities like Iceland with a population a little over a quarter of a million strong. Nor does size appear to inhibit a community from demanding separation from its neighbours, as did Anguilla from St Kitts-Nevis. Similarly in Africa, ethnic communities of different size and scale may demand greater autonomy or independence; and while some like the Konzo in Uganda or Chagga in Tanzania, may be quite small, others like the Ibo, Mandingo, BaKongo, Xhosa and Somali may run into the hundreds of thousands or even millions and become thus eminently 'viable' for nationhood.[34]

Considerations of this kind have prompted some scholars to stress the similarities between African 'tribalism' and European 'nationalism' more than their superficial differences. Argyle, for example, has argued that many African 'tribes' are really no different from their European 'ethnic' counterparts, and their collective aspirations also mirror those of European nationalisms. 'Tribalism' in Africa is really nothing more nor less than the aspiration to turn an ethnic community into a fully-fledged 'nation' enjoying maximum autonomy or in-dependence.[35] And he cites several examples including the Kikuyu, Ibo, Yoruba, Zulu and BaKongo; the latter, too, formed their own ethnic party in the Belgian Congo in 1952, the ABAKO, partly to rediscover and preserve ethnic culture, partly to advance their social and political interests in Leo-poldville, in this as in other features paralleling their European counterparts.[36]

What Argyle here terms 'tribalism', I have called 'ethnicism' which may eventuate in an outright 'ethnic nationalism'. The term 'tribalism', like 'tribe' itself, has become largely a poli-tical epithet, used by the leaders of new states to justify the suppression of ethnic cleavages or their manifestations in the political arena. By designating such ethnic solidarities and sentiments as so much 'tribalism', the leaders of the new states can dispute the 'ethnic' label and consign ethnic activity to an 'archaic' stage of society or to the colonial past, in the name of avoiding 'balkanisation' and centrifugal tendencies.[37] For where 'tribalism' can be justifiably denigrated, genuine 'ethnicism', once conceded, must be tolerated and accomm-odated; hence the policies, alluded to earlier, of 'ethnic arith-metic', in which social services, employment facilities and economic resources are distributed on the basis of ethnic numerical proportions of the total population.[38] An example of this occurred in 1968 in Kenya, where, to meet objections by peripheral ethnic communities and small tribes against excessive 'Kikuyuisation' of central governmental and other posts and facilities, a commission was appointed which recommended a more equitable proportional redistribution of goods and services and fairer employment practices to help the disadvantaged groups; for the adoption of purely 'universa-listic' and 'achievement' criteria will always benefit dispro-portionately the centrally placed and more advantaged groups in any state. The Kenyan Parliament, however, rejected the commission's recommendations, despite grim allusions on the floor to the struggle then raging in Biafra.[39]

Once 'ethnicism' is conceded (and scholars are divided on how to characterise and separate it from 'tribalism'), the way is clear to a more complex view of African nationalism and the

concept of an African 'nation'. For it then becomes obvious
that African nationalism can operate, simultaneously in some
cases, at three distinct levels: that of the ethnic community, the
community of history and culture, which gives rise to 'ethnic
nationalism'; that of the state, the heir of the colonial territory,
a 'political community' based on territorial definition, and
giving rise to a 'territorial nationalism'; and finally that of the
continent as a whole, or at least the sub-Saharan part of it, a
community of colour and colonial experience, giving rise to a
'Pan' nationalism of all Africans. None of these levels is
mutually exclusive; they may at times come into conflict, but
then 'dual' or 'triple' loyalties are quite common in today's
world and they may operate quite satisfactorily as 'concentric
circles of allegiance', in Coleman's term;[40] a man may feel
himself to be a Kikuyu, a Kenyan and an African, and his
choice of 'national' identity will depend largely upon the context in which he is placed.

In fact, the common practice of opposing 'ethnicism' (or
pejoratively 'tribalism') to 'territorialism' and devaluing the
former as 'subnationalism' and reserving for the latter alone
the honoured title of 'nationalism', overlooks the vital, if
indirect, contribution that ethnic nationalism can, and has
made, to the growth and persistence of territorial state-wide
nationalisms. We have already seen how ethnic re-classification in the new urban setting helped African immigrants by
providing them with new ties and by enabling them thereby to
mobilise for social and political purposes. In the African
context, this meant that the new associations that were constituted in the towns acted as mutual self-help organisations of
a voluntary kind, in such matters as employment opportunities, insurance and welfare services, burial societies, clubs
and the like. These associations, formed on the basis often of
earlier 'tribal' affiliations, but actually, as we saw, reflecting a
new ethnic alignment which drew on the past for quite
modern purposes, afforded a ready-made base for political
parties and societies, and became the springboard for those
coalitions of ethnic communities which helped to force out the
colonial powers and won independence for the whole territory. In that sense, ethnicism contributed to the force and
cohesion of the territorial movements for independence.[41]

What about the role of ethnicism after independence? From constituting an important plank and component of the movement for independence, has it now become a threat to that independence and state-wide unity, as so many assert? There is little doubt that, in a few cases, these fears have proved correct, though rather less often than one might expect from the volume and gravity of the fears expressed. Cases like Biafra, Eritrea and Kurdistan should not blind us to the fact that, in a much greater number of cases, ethnic communities have not demanded independence and have accommodated their desires for greater autonomy to the existing state framework and its economic resources, as they do in Europe today.[42] As with the Scots or Catalans, sober economic reasons may well help to mute secessionist aspirations, as may the fear of military incapacity. But there is another side to the role of 'ethnicism' in the new states. In these 'state-nations' (states aspiring to become nations), the conflicting pressures set up by a multiplicity of ethnic communities — and many African and some Asian states contain more than two ethnic groupings — actually serve to reinforce the control of the state and so ensure its otherwise rather fragile unity. This is particularly the case where ethnic cleavages do not correspond with economic or class antagonisms; by cross-cutting economic differentials, ethnic ties mute incipient class conflict and bolster the overall power of the central organs of state. Where, on the other hand, ethnic communities are also aligned along class lines, or perhaps feel they are victims of economic discrimination, the chances for ethnic revolt are multiplied; even then, however, the chances of success in a war of secession are blunted by the tendency for the great powers not to intervene on their behalf, or indeed actively to discourage secession, and by the trend for the other ethnic communities to unite against the dissident ethnic community and rally to the central state. Acts of would-be separation, like that of the Lunda in Shaba province, suppressed with French help, run foul of international opinion and local opposition; thus the very multiplicity of ethnic communities, and of their differing relationships with the bureaucratic state, help to ensure the survival of existing territorial 'post-colonial' states.[43]

Here, again, we encounter the enormous influence of

Western models of national formation. Essentially, these are 'statist' models: European nations, in the Western half of the continent, were, to a considerable extent, the creation of states and state-makers. State-making preceded nation-forming in the West, and was its crucible in Spain, France, England, Sweden and even Holland. It was this set of models, rather than the Eastern European ones, in which the 'nation', already well formed, became the mould and measure of the state, that has in the past acted as the major influence and constraint on African national development, and continues to do so today.[44] Both at the economic and political levels, the major powers, East and West, will only deal with and operate through the prism of the 'state-nation', the only recognised constituent of the inter-state system of which they are the acknowledged leaders, and which they themselves embody and understand. In that political sense, indeed, Marx's dictum has stood the test of time:

The country that is more developed industrially only shows to the less developed, the image of its own future.[45]

*　　*　　*

African societies today, we may conclude, are clearly and deeply divided along ethnic lines, even though in many cases ethnicism may actually reinforce the control, if not the stability, of the post-colonial state. African politics is often ethnic politics, and its major internal economic issues are ethnic rather than simply class ones. Does this mean, then, that class and class conflict are still irrelevant in Africa today? Can we not detect the basis of a new class society emerging in the African continent?

It might be thought that a discussion of the other great potential divide in contemporary African and Asian societies was freer of terminological and political problems than that of ethnicity. But this is to overlook the very Western provenance of the language of class. Marxist conceptions of class conflict are, after all, rooted in a Western European historical experience; and terms like petty bourgeoisie, which are drawn from mid-19th century French society, can hardly be applied indiscriminately to African and Asian societies in the 20th century. In the absence of an African Marx, we need to proceed, therefore, with particular caution.

The first question concerns the nature and present relevance of pre-colonial divisions in Africa and Asia. In the classic marxist schema, these pre-capitalist formations are generally dubbed 'feudal', although today marxist scholars are showing a greater sensitivity to the range of 'pre-capitalist' (or better 'non-capitalist') formations.[46] Nevertheless, a number of scholars in that tradition would adhere to the traditional view that the pre-capitalist stage in Africa, as elsewhere, was one of 'feudalism'.[47] Of course, not all social groupings and societies on the African (or Asian) continent had reached that stage; some 'hunting-and-gathering' tribes remained in a stage of almost primitive communism, while in others the ownership and control of land was vested in the community itself, being of a 'tribal' character, as that term was understood by the 19th century anthropologists like von Maurer and Morgan whom Marx and Engels most leaned upon.[48] In both cases, as in the great Asiatic despotisms, class differentiation was almost entirely absent, and the same was true of many medieval African states. Nevertheless, elements of European feudalism clearly were present in some African state systems prior to the advent of colonialism. Among the Nupe studied by Nadel, the feudal lords or *egba* possessed land fiefs or *tunga* and raised military forces for the king from among their personal clients. Indeed the institution of *bara* or clientship was fairly widespread in northern Nigeria; and even vassalage, together with the fief, was found by M.G. Smith in the Hausa state of Zaria.[49] Elsewhere, feudal elements can also be found. In Ruanda, Maquet reported the institution of clientship, not only among the dominant Tutsi but even among the subordinate Hutu agriculturalists, although the loan of cattle took the place of the land fief.[50] Among the Ganda in Uganda, and the Ashanti in Ghana, there were groups of big landowners; and Lucy Mair has analysed the position of the territorial chiefs in Buganda, who did not, however, secure personal services from their subordinate peasantry.[51]

These cases seem, however, to have been atypical; and for this and other reasons, Jack Goody in a highly sophisticated analysis, wishes to deny the appellation 'feudalism' to most African societies, with the exception of the Ethiopian empire. He does not deny that several complex African 'state' societies possessed some 'feudal' features, notably clientship and the fief; but he shows that very few approximated the whole European or Japanese syndrome of features in their entirety. He argues that there were few real landlords in the European sense, only 'lords of the land', who owed their economic position, not to their ownership or control of the means of production, but of the means of destruction. This did not preclude considerable differences in life-styles between strata, particularly in West Africa; but the distinction rested upon possession of the means of domination through war, most notably the horse and the gun. Besides, African technology did not match the European; it had no wheel or plough, and therefore employed shifting cultivation of land that was, after all, plentiful; which in turn implied that land was not such a vital element in the economy.[52] For all these reasons, the African pattern of development does not fit the European experience of feudalism, and hence of its unique transition to capitalism.

This is not the place to enter into a discussion of the validity of Goody's analysis. Suffice it to say that, even on his own evidence, some important African societies might well be termed semi-feudal or 'feudaloid', rather like the Balkan provinces of the Ottoman empire; the key element of exploitation and protection of the peasantry by an armed stratum of cavalry warriors, with or without a hierarchy of fiefs, did obtain in these societies.[53] There were also important differences. Slavery rather than serfdom was a feature of several empires and states, as was tribute-collecting and raids for booty; nor was there the same cultural distance between nobility and peasantry as came to exist in Europe. In this respect, 'tribal' and ethnic loyalty had a more long-lasting and egalitarian influence.

How far have the pre-colonial ethnic elites, the old chiefly families, been able to retain their hold on people's loyalties in the countryside and use their influence to obtain power in the new urban centres? Is there a considerable measure of continuity between the new elites and the old chiefly ones? Again, scholars are sharply divided. Some like Coleman, Kimble and Lloyd tend to regard the new urban elites as having superseded the old ruling families and traditional chiefs, and to have opted for modernisation and innovation against the forces of tradition and conservatism.[54] Others — Kilson, Fallers, Markovitz — stress the continuity between the old ruling strata and the new, regarding such changes as have occurred in the 'ruling class' as institutional rather than structural. In other words, the old rulers have simply adapted to the new bureaucratic and commercial institutions of the urban setting in the new states.[55]

Once again, the evidence can be used to support both points of view, depending on the states selected. In some areas — northern Nigeria, Senegal, Ethiopia, in Uganda, Niger and Sierra Leone — traditional ruling strata, usually chiefs and their families, have managed to retain much of their old powers, although they have had to shift their power base to the towns, exchanging their traditional roles in the rural 'tribe' for the new ones of the urban ethnic association, and their ritual and customary status for administrative power and commercial wealth.[56] On the other side, new openings in commerce and the professions, as well as administration, have given many more opportunities to commoners; conversely, these new institutions have attracted many sons of chiefs who acquired Western education, to fight against the traditional powers of their own families and stratum, in favour of the new social order in which they themselves have won a power base. Hence they stand in the forefront of the fight by the representatives of the new state to subordinate all local and traditional powers to itself. So, in western Nigeria, we find Awolowo acquiring an honorary chieftaincy in 1954, while the Yoruba chiefs prepared to work with the new strata and their Action Group, and similarly among the Ibo; and even in socialist Tanzania, where the chieftaincy as an institution was dissolved, members of the ruling TANU party elite were often drawn from better-off, educated, but traditional families, whose acquisition of Western education in colonial schools inspired them with the desire to eradicate the last vestiges of traditional authority.[57]

On one point, both sides in this argument are in agreement. This is that the new towns have thrown up new elites and strata — wealthy cash-crop farmers, businessmen and managers, workers and intelligentsia — none of which had pre-colonial roots; and further, that these new elites formed political associations and parties and constituted the driving force behind the movement for independence and national integration after independence. The question is: how far can these strata be called 'classes', in the structural sense of that term? How far have they emerged from the penetration of capitalism, and to what extent has such an externally-based exchange capitalism succeeded in producing an internal class division in African societies, like that which endogenous capitalism produced in Europe?

These are large questions, and I propose to confine my comments to the emergence of a wage-earning proletariat, since that is an indispensable definitional element of capitalism itself. How large and self-conscious of its class status is the working-class in African societies? How far does it act in accordance with its postulated 'class interests'? (The question of the 'class nature' of the ruling strata will be examined in the next chapter).[58]

The evidence for the size and solidarity of the working-class in African societies is both patchy and conflicting. There are countries with a definite proletariat – Kenya, Zambia and Zimbabwe, Zaire – but, with the exception of the former Belgian Congo, even here it is relatively small as a percentage of the total working population, usually well under 10%, or 12% if we include migrant labour.[59] A good many uprooted migrants are unemployed and live in the slum areas of the new, or old, towns. The strength of trades union, too, vary greatly; they have been powerful forces in the Sudan, Guinea, Mali, Nigeria, Kenya and Zambia, though only in the first three did the unions participate in politics, that is, as the radical wing of a 'mass' nationalism (as they did also in Tunisia). In most cases, they preferred the path of 'economism', dealing with pay and working conditions mainly, and only rarely being manipulated or appealed to by the nationalist parties.[60]

On the other hand, there is some evidence of a growing class identification in those centres where a wage-earning proletariat is concentrated for long periods. Originally, workers in the Zambian (then Rhodesian) copperbelt in the 1940s, were organised by the white managers and owners along tribal lines, and tribal leaders were appointed or brought in to act as their spokesmen and to convey the needs of authority. But, in his classic study, Epstein showed how, as confrontations over pay and conditions with the white bosses increased, the workers became more and more conscious of their class position, and their demands took on a greater class orientation. They soon ejected their tribal elders, on which the managers and government had relied, and proceeded to appoint their own union spokesmen, uniting as workers rather than along ethnic lines. Their 'tribal' affiliation, admittedly foisted on them by external agencies, was perceived as a tool of alien authority, and became an irrelevance (or positively harmful) in the new social setting.[61] In this, as in other cases from South Africa and Nigeria, we find a growing proletariat, once it is concentrated and becomes conscious of its powers, forsaking its traditional 'tribal' affiliations for class ones; and that is a pattern which observers like Lerner's team found elsewhere, in this case, in the Middle East.[62]

Does this mean that we should expect class interests to supersede those of ethnic communities, as capitalist industrialism penetrates the African continent, and that the workers will be the first to make this exchange of group loyalties? Not entirely. Indeed, if we were to extrapolate from present tendencies, the likelihood of such a supersession is fairly remote; and that, for several interrelated reasons.

To begin with, though both ethnic communities and classes are present on the African (and Asian) scene, the former are much stronger and more widespread than the latter, except perhaps among the small minority of wage workers. Whereas ethnic ties remain a powerful force in African societies, class formation is far less well developed, with some exceptions, and class conflict of the kind familiar in Europe is still relatively infrequent, its place being taken by ethnic conflicts or by elite rivalries or political repression by the state bureaucracy.

In the second place, industrialisation is very patchy over the continent as a whole. Capitalism, in the stricter sense of capitalist relations of production, is still not very widespread in Africa (rather more so in parts of Asia, like India and Malaysia), although most of the continent is now bound to commercial exchange relations with the West, its primary products feeding the world market and the advanced industrial economies of the metropolitan states.[63] In some African states, however, — notably Zaire, Kenya, Uganda and Nigeria — the great multi-national companies have put down their financial and economic roots in the indigenous society, or at any rate its urban sector; and here we find signs of class formation, though this is inhibited by the presence of powerful metropolitan bourgeoisie which overshadows the chances of a native bourgeoisie, just as the use of expatriate managers helped to delay for a time the growth of an African managerial class. To the degree to which the metropolitan bourgeoisie, however, needs an indigenous one to provide domestic capital for its local operations, an African bourgeoisie is coming into being, though it tends to be more of a trading entrepreneurial class than an industrial bourgeoisie; for the introduction of heavy industry on the north European pattern has been questioned as a means to rapid development, in favour of greater reliance on agricultural diversification and on local light industries. Once again, this means that tropical Africa has (with some exceptions) tended not to follow the European model of concentrations of workers in large factories producing heavy industrial goods.[64]

Thirdly, there has been a greater continuity between old and traditional ruling strata and recent elites than we find in much of Continental Europe or America, and this has ensured the persistence of ethnic affiliations. So, too, does the existence of a huge reservoir of peasants, territorially dispersed yet available for mobilisation in certain conditions, and feeding the new towns with waves of migrant labour or immigrants, who can then be 're-classified' by their ethnic origin and culture and history, and used as a weapon in the political arena of the principal cities. So, there are always new recruits to the ethnic banner; the very malleability of 'tribal' affiliation, of the new kind of ethnicity, helps to keep it alive. Like the caste associations in India, 'tribal' affiliation, now become ethnicism, has shown that it can be adapted to quite new conditions and take on a different life, guiding the individual in his identity problems and serving as a social focus for his interests and attachments. Thus the rejuvenation of ethnicity, fed by this continuity with older elites and the waves of peasant migration, tends to inhibit the development of classes based upon purely economic and property relations, such as

were found in modern Europe; other types of social relationship, based upon interests and ties that did not stem from
purely productive relations, have taken priority in the African
context and have then helped to diminish and circumscribe the
importance of class interests and formations.

These considerations must, then, lead us to the inevitable
conclusion that it is purely Europocentric to imagine that
'classes' must supersede 'ethnic communities'. Such continental myopia is only reinforced by the common, but misleading, equation of ethnic groups and sentiments with 'tribal'
ones, and of 'tribalism' with 'ethnicism'. If we drop this identification, we can immediately see that, even in Europe itself, as
well as North America to this day, class formation, though
deep and extensive, has not superseded ethnicity as a social
force. On the contrary: we are today witnessing a resurgence
of ethnicism in Europe itself and in Canada, not to mention the
'symbolic ethnicity' found in the United States. Class conflict
exists today side by side with ethnic autonomism in the many
'plural' states of the West, interacting in a sort of counterpoint
relationship. There is no reason to think that they may not do
likewise in Africa and Asia, or that classes will somehow
undermine ethnic communities in the not too distant future.
On present evidence, it is most unlikely.[65]

5 State and Intelligentsia

One of the major weaknesses of both modernisation and marxist paradigms is their failure to provide an adequate and convincing account of the current position and role of the intelligentsia, especially in the 'Third World'. Of itself, this would create an important lacuna in any general theory; but this omission is the more damaging because a good case can be made out for the proposition that today's ruling stratum in the new states of Africa and Asia is drawn from the personnel, and follows the interests, of the intelligentsia, and that particular civilian and military regimes are likewise formed from circles of the intelligentsia and act on their behalf, even more than that of other strata. It is this proposition, and its significance for the new states, that this chapter examines.

The relative neglect of the intelligentsia by the major paradigms has been increasingly redressed in the work of several scholars, who are dissatisfied with traditional formulations. Following the lead of Karl Mannheim, they have sought to link major social and political changes with the rise and nature of 'Third World' intelligentsia.[1] J.H. Kautsky, indeed, considers them to be the main beneficiaries of colonial rule, while at the same time constituting its leading opponents. Designating them 'intellectuals' rather than intelligentsia, Kautsky places them at the head of a triple alliance of new strata in underdeveloped countries, the others being the workers and the native bourgeoisies. Each of these strata is treated as an 'interest group' in its own right; but the interests of the intellectuals are at present preponderant, because the other two new strata are weak and undeveloped, and are as yet overshadowed by the power of the metropolitan bourgeoisies. For this reason, the intellectuals must take the lead, both in opposing colonialism and in leading the country towards the goals of modernisation. By 'modernisation', Kautsky means essentially industrialisation and its trappings, including the skills and values of more advanced societies in the West. The intellectuals have assimilated these skills and values, and so desire westernisation and modernisation, but free of Western interference; they oppose traditionalism, and its native guardians, their own aristocracies, and seek to eject the colonial powers, while retaining their technology and values. Kautsky explains this ambivalence in terms of their local situation: intellectuals are usually under-employed and culturally displaced in their own societies, and so their nationalism becomes an expression of their drive for rapid modernisation independent of foreign tutelage.[2] Economically, their modernising nationalism faces both ways: it opposes the new economic order of capitalism, yet at the same time scorns purely agricultural development based on the old order and its time-honoured representatives, the peasant masses, preferring rapid industrialisation, planned and executed through state controls. This accounts for their tendency towards a more socialistic type of nationalism and their deepseated ambivalence towards the West; a theme to which I return in the next chapter.[3]

While Kautsky's account emphasised the economic determinants of the intelligentsia and their nationalism, some might say at the expense of the cultural and political dimensions, that of Ernest Gellner highlights the seminal role of linguistic culture and the effects of literacy. Gellner, too, stresses the role of the intelligentsia today, regarding them as one of the two prongs of the nationalist movements, the other being the proletariat. The reason for their prominence Gellner attributes to the uneven and eroding effects of industrialisation and modernisation, as it sweeps out from its Western heartlands. Because it undermines traditional role structures, modernisation brings cultural bonds and linguistic communication to the fore; language and culture become the new kinds of social cement, and that puts a premium on literacy and 'clerkly' education in a particular language. To accommodate an educational system capable of turning out large numbers of literate and numerate people, a national state is required; and it becomes the cultural, as well as material, interest of the intelligentsia to promote the cause of national secession and independence.[4]

Gellner's account of the intelligentsia appears in the context of his broader theory of nationalism, which is held to be a sociologically necessary concomitant of modernisation. It can be objected that such an argument presupposes a functional 'fit' between the needs of an industrial system, which is often only embryonic when nationalism first appears in a society, a certain level and kind of educational attainment, a unified language and a certain 'nation-sized' scale, and that these elements rarely co-vary in the way postulated by the theory.[5] However, even if Gellner's explanation of nationalism and nations proves teleological or otherwise inadequate, his account of the pivotal role of the intelligentsia and their cultural interests, has proved both influential and rewarding. It has helped to stimulate interest in the situation and activities of intelligentsia, just as Shils' earlier studies of the intellectuals helped to focus attention on their crucial functions in the new states.[6] Recently, indeed, some of these themes have been taken up by Alvin Gouldner in some 'theses' on the New Class of intellectuals who, Gouldner alleges, are fast replacing the dying bourgeoisies of the West. Gouldner briefly traces their social history, to find them now firmly entrenched as experts in 'line' bureaucracies, and challenging the domination of the bureaucrats themselves. For Gouldner, the New Class, though subdivided into 'humanistic intellectuals' and 'technical intelligentsia', constitute a definite 'class', because they share a common culture of critical discourse and reproduce jointly a common fund of cultural capital. It is they, rather than the revolutionary workers, who in every land are increasingly taking over the functions of a ruling class, especially as advanced technology accelerates the growth and rise of technical experts.[7] Although Gouldner says little about 'Third World' intellectuals, or about nation-states, his general approach represents a clear advance over traditional neglect of this stratum; and although one might take issue with the class language in which his theses are cast, their substance is clearly relevant to the reality of political change in the new states and converges with several of the positions adopted here.

For in Africa and Asia today it has become abundantly clear that the apex of the new status system and the new political order — and on this most observers are in agreement — is occupied by the intelligentsia, who thereby have become the leading political stratum in most of the new states. Indeed, if we define the intelligentsia as the professional strata, both humanistic and technical, including such occupations as lawyers, doctors, journalists, academics, school-teachers, economists, architects and planners, technicians and engineers, indeed experts of every kind, all those who have had some form of tertiary education and utilise their educational certificates to secure access to high-status occupations and earn their livelihood on the basis of their diplomas and their vocational training; if we treat the intelligentsia as the disseminators and appliers of ideas and paradigms created and analysed by the much smaller circles of 'intellectuals', then in Africa today the professionals make up a definite stratum from which political leaders are recruited, and which the latter tend to represent and whose interests they support.[8] It would be simplistic to claim that the intelligentsia constitute the sole political stratum; but they are undoubtedly the leading such stratum, especially if we include the military among the modern professionals. Professional occupations tend to be over-represented in both the legislative and executive branches of government; in his analysis of post-independence African legislatures, Guy Hunter found a disproportionate number of lawyers, teachers and other professional groups as deputies and leading politicians, while traders and business-men played only a very secondary role.[9] The Smythes, too, in their early study of the Nigerian political elite, found that most political leaders in that country were drawn from professional groups — notably teachers, journalists and lawyers — while businessmen were under-represented.[10] Others, too, have found that western education was the chief criterion distinguishing those with political power in African states today; the professionals turned out to be the chief beneficiaries of the 'post-colonial' state, their very use of the term 'elite' helping to set them apart.[11] High-prestige occupations such as law and medicine attract children of educated parents, not simply for their intrinsic or social worth, but for the political chances they proffer.[12] University training is increasingly viewed as the main channel of political mobility, a prerequisite for elite status and a bureaucratic or political career; for all their egalitarian rhetoric, university students tend to identify closely with the models of the educational system and the civil service, seeing in both channels for political advancement, and rightly so.[13] Even within present-day one-party or military regimes, the intelligentsia remain firmly entrenched in the political and administrative apparatus as the indispensable instrument of rule; the officers have, on the whole, had little option but to retain the professionals as the only political 'experts', the only stratum capable of ensuring the smooth and orderly functioning of government and the economy in contemporary African states.

How shall we characterise this new political stratum of professional intelligentsia? Do they correspond in any way to the familiar western patterns of a bourgeois 'ruling class'? Can we likewise ascribe their rise to the growth of capitalism and industry? That is, broadly speaking, the standpoint adopted in the recent analysis of class and power in Africa by Irving Leonard Markovitz.[14] He claims that what I have here termed the professional intelligentsia can be described as an 'organisational bourgeoisie'; distinguishable from the mass of their compatriots by their appearance and life-style, this organisational bourgeoisie occupy 'strategic locations' in society and so are able to make decisions affecting the lives of tens of thousands of their fellow-citizens, while they themselves live off the 'national income'. And Markovitz defines them as follows:

In this book, I use the term *organisational bourgeoisie* to refer to a combined ruling group consisting of the top political leaders and bureaucrats, the traditional rulers and their descendants, and the leading members of the liberal professions and the rising business bourgeoisie. Top members of the military and police forces are also part of this bureaucratic bourgeoisie. Over time, leading elements in this coalition change. Although the bureaucratic and political components have dominated until now, they have had to seek a social base. Increasingly in West African countries, as in independent countries on the continent everywhere, a developing commercial and business class provides that base.[15]

Markovitz is, in effect, making two assertions here; first, that this coalition acts as a bourgeoisie, albeit an organisational one, in terms of the privileges it acquires and the life-style and education it possesses which set it apart from the rest of the population; and second, that the social base of the position of this bureaucratic and political ruling class is provided by a developing commercial and business class.

Both these contentions are open to criticism. Can we, in the first instance, term such a coalition of disparate groups a 'class', let alone a 'bourgeoisie'? Certainly not in the traditional marxist sense of that term; too many discrepant elements, deriving their position and privileges from a variety of sources, make up Markovitz's 'organisational bourgeoisie'. In no sense of the term can such a 'combined ruling group' be described as a single economic 'class' of bourgeois; leading members of the liberal professions and top members of the police forces or civil service cannot, by any stretch of the imagination, be classed with owners of large-scale capital or commodity producers or employers of wage-labour.[16] In fact, the term 'organisational bourgeoisie' is a hybrid, attempting to unify often conflicting elements within a western-derived scheme, whose applicability to the African context remains hypothetical. True, the various elites that Markovitz lists, all have much greater access to wealth, education and various privileges than the vast mass of peasants; and neither is social mobility as great as has been thought. But both access and mobility are more a function of political position than strictly economic occupations and activities. It is their control of office within party machines, government and civil service that confers wealth and privilege upon so many who otherwise would have had little access to them, just as it is the use of political leverage and controls that regulates, and restricts, social mobility from below into the elites themselves. To transfer a European scheme like that of the marxist 'ruling class' to the African context, even with the 'organisational' modification introduced by Markovitz, misses this vital difference in which the European causal chain is reversed in Africa today, and economic privileges are often a result, rather than the cause, of political power in the new states. As for the future, to assume that the present causal nexus will be reversed again to conform to the European pattern (because economic bases of power are more stable in the long-term than political ones), neglects other features peculiar to Africa, such as the vitality of ethnic ties and organisation, which are likely to mitigate the effects of class formation and provide alternative bases of power for decades to come.[17]

On the second issue, the social rooting of the 'organisational bourgeoisie', Markovitz does indeed present evidence for the select nature of the old African elites under early colonial rule. These original urban elites were drawn from the sons of chiefs and other 'tribal' notables who had migrated to the city at the end of the 19th century, and who constituted the old urban elites, a rather exclusive set of families, often contemptuous of the poor, the uneducated and the mass of inhabitants in the interior of the Gold Coast, Sierra Leone, Nigeria or Senegal, of all those who did not benefit from colonial rule like themselves.[18] But we cannot really call these old exclusive and wealthy elites the emergent African bourgeoisie presiding over the growth of African capitalism. Though many of them were engaged in overseas trade, there was nothing peculiarly capitalistic in their activities; at most they became partially involved in a purely *exchange* and distributive capitalism, but without any capitalist *relations of production* emerging under their auspices within the continent itself. They did not employ any large-scale wage-labour force, nor revolutionise the instruments of production. Moreover, the new elites that emerged after the Second World War were only partly linked with these older urban elites; many of the new men were drawn from poorer sections of the population and educated in the new government schools and colleges, some of them working their way as students overseas.[19] Partly for these reasons, they did not necessarily identify with the interests of the older urban elites and their colonial mentors, and in fact soon adopted more radical policies which shocked their elders and threatened the position of the old elites as well as the tribal chiefs.[20] Nor can we assume a complete identity of interests between the new educated elites and the rising business class and newly trained managers in Africa. Even family connections did not ensure a common perception of unitary 'class interests'. Since independence, it is true, many African leaders have had to reckon with the influence of a 'business lobby', along with that of the trades union, in the political arena; but, in itself, that says little about the social roots of the professional intelligentsia or their perceptions of common interests. Besides, the African business class has, with some exceptions, proved to be much smaller than its European counterparts and far more restricted in its operations; the real factor with which the new political stratum must reckon is not the local African bourgeoisie, but the powerful metropolitan bourgeoisies and their multi-national corporations.[21]

It does not, therefore, help our enquiry into the character of the African professional intelligentsia and their novel political role to define it as an 'organisational bourgeoisie', or to locate its social origins and power base within a rather small and recent African business class, itself so overshadowed by a far more advanced metropolitan bourgeoisie. For it is really its 'organisational' component that distinguishes this stratum, whereas the analogy with a European bourgeoisie tends to be misleading; while, on the other hand, the penetration of capitalism throughout Africa has, as we saw, been inter-mittent and patchy in character, and only recently and in certain areas has it had any lasting impact upon the nature of purely productive, as opposed to exchange, relations.

How, then, shall we explain the position and role of the African professional intelligentsia, and their assumption of power today? It is usual in such investigations to link their role with the rise of commercial capitalism and processes of economic development, and even to derive political change from these economic factors. Without denying the influence of such factors, the attempt to derive political changes from purely economic developments runs into both the definitional and the historical difficulties we encountered above; and, more important, it tends to overlook the effects of prior changes within the political and ideological spheres themselves. But these spheres can, I think, furnish us with alternative accounts of the role and political position of the intelligentsia; and in what follows I should like to consider two such alternatives which complement each other, and 'fill out' the account of their role which would otherwise become too schematic and undeveloped.

The first of these lines of argument centres on the relations between the intelligentsia and the bureaucratic state itself. Here we examine in greater detail the 'organisational' component of Markovitz's dual characterisation. The present strategic role of the professional intelligentsia derives, in part, from the needs and circumstances of colonial rule. It is worth recalling those circumstances. We saw earlier that colonial rule derived its special character from the nature of its origins as a political 'export' from its European progenitors. That is to say, the colonial state as a variant of the modern European state, took on the character of a decapitated version of its European models: a highly centralised and territorially clearly demarcated set of public institutions, autonomous and differentiated from other social institutions, and wielding the monopoly of coercion and extraction of resources within its territorial domain. In a word, the gubernatorial and bureaucratic state, enforcing its commands through an exclusive civilian and military apparatus of power. But, as the colonial state became more deeply entrenched and expanded the scale and scope of its operations, it needed more qualified and better trained personnel to staff its lower and middle ranks and execute its policies in an orderly and cost-effective manner. So the bureaucratic state came to rely more and more, as it had previously in Europe, on large numbers of clerks in junior positions and growing bodies of 'experts' in the middle ranks and in various auxiliary institutions.[22] Experts, of course, were distinguished by their technical competence and professionalism; and for some time the colonial administrations could rely on metropolitan experts for the relevant skills and attitudes. But, as the colonial state began to intervene in more and more sectors of society and inaugurate social changes, it had to supplement its own experts and clerks with new recruits from Africa itself. And, since at the time there was a dearth of the relevant expertise in African societies, colonial governments felt increasingly compelled to found secondary schools, colleges and institutes like the William Ponty School or Achimota College, in order to train suitable African personnel or to encourage African youth to acquire the necessary skills and attitudes in European and American universities.[23] These qualified Africans could then be admitted to the lower ranks of the governmental bureaucracies, or attached as experts to bodies of expatriates in auxiliary institutions.

These were the educated elites who soon began to agitate for national independence after the Second World War, and who aimed to wrest the top posts within the bureaucracies for themselves.

And, in due course, within the overall process of decolonisation, from which many African strata benefited, the elite of qualified professionals or intelligentsia, did indeed come to inherit the leading bureaucratic and political positions in the 'post–colonial' state. In a sense the whole edifice of the colonial state fell into their hands. And as it was highly developed and had become a powerful mechanism of control, this same colonial state, despite its recent appearance and social fragility, became the bastion and power base for the intelligentsia. In the West, the aspiring experts and professionals are still struggling to be accepted in many public institutions run by old-line bureaucrats; whereas in Africa, the professional intelligentsia, because of the sudden departure of the colonial bureaucrats, were able to seize most of the top positions and eliminate their rivals for political power at independence. In this way, professionals and intellectuals succeeded to a position of unparalleled power in the 'post–colonial' state.[24]

These developments are by no means confined to Africa. In some Asian states, too, the professionalised bureaucracy has become a crucial factor in the political struggles and occupies a strategic role after independence. In Pakistan, for example, Alavi distinguished three propertied classes — the native landowners and bourgeoisie, and the metropolitan bourgeoisie — and found that none of them was able to constitute a ruling class.[25] Being relatively weak by Western standards, they required the support and favour of the 'post–colonial' state and its bureaucratic-military apparatus to further their respective interests. Alavi explains that this situation stemmed from the requirements of colonialism. Colonial rulers need a mechanism by means of which they can stand above the societies they control. Colonialism, therefore, has to

create a state apparatus (in the colony) through which it can exercise dominion over *all* the indigenous social classes in the colony. It might be said that the 'superstructure' in the colony is, therefore, 'overdeveloped' in relation to the 'structure' in the colony, for its basis lies in the metropolitan structure itself, from which it is later separated at the time of independence. The colonial state is therefore equipped with a powerful bureaucratic-military apparatus and mechanisms of government which enable them through its routine operations to subordinate the native social classes.[26]

There is a second reason for the greater strength of the post-colonial state: its role in economic development after independence. The post-colonial state

directly appropriates a very large part of the economic surplus and deploys it in bureaucratically directed economic activity in the name of promoting economic development.[27]

As a result, the new states are not only more powerful than their respective 'civil societies'; their bureaucratic staff, civilian and military, enjoy unmatched political and economic power.

In fact, compared to most African states, the class structure and institutional development of states like Pakistan is more advanced. In Africa, the distance between state and society is, in one sense, even greater: the indigenous bourgeoisie is tiny, and the landowning classes are either rudimentary or, in settler societies, of white European extraction.[28] This is particularly the case in East Africa, where John Saul has applied some of Alavi's analysis, and found that these differences give the post-colonial state even greater powers and room for manoeuvre. At the same time, given the relative lack of capitalist development in Kenya, Uganda and Tanzania, especially the latter, the state finds that it must actually *create* those territorial and ideological conditions which can foster capitalism in East Africa, and allow the rise of a hegemonic bourgeoisie, which till now had been stifled by the Asian commercial classes.[29]

The great merit of Alavi's formulations, applied to Africa, is to draw attention to the formidable powers of the military and bureaucratic elements controlling the state apparatus, of which there has been so much evidence in both east and west Africa. To a large degree, these professional and bureaucratic elements can act with little reference to the interests of emergent social classes, though a good deal less *vis-a-vis* ethnic interests. The post-colonial state and its bureaucracy is relatively autonomous of civil society; it possesses a fairly 'free hand', a phrase that the Tanzanian socialist, Issa Shivji, applies to the 'bureaucratic bourgeoisie' and its control of the state, to characterise a stratum that has cut itself off from its original petty bourgeois base.[30] It is this free hand which allows the intelligentsia to use its control over the state apparatus to gain economic privileges otherwise beyond them, with the result that it no longer requires a base in civil society; its base, as we said, has become the organs of state, its qualifications are its educational certificates, and its role is that of an autonomous and leading political stratum, able to make alliances or break them at its choosing. From which it follows that the chief political struggles in Africa today, including ethnic ones, are at root factional conflicts within the intelligentsia – civilian versus military, liberal versus marxist, regional or ethnic conflicts – and that any involvement on the part of other strata or classes is at the invitation or behest of one or other faction within the ruling stratum of the intelligentsia.[31] The only real challenges posed to the hegemony of the intelligentsia come from the metropolitan bourgeoisie (Alavi's native bourgeoisies and landowners are either too small or absent in Africa), and, less often, from their working and peasant classes. Within the severe constraints of the 'grid' of territorial states, within the bounds of the global interstate system and the client-blocs of the superpowers, with *their* dominant classes and political elites, the African intelligentsia has become the politically strategic stratum, because it alone commands the institutional heights of the post-colonial state, of which it has been the chief creation and beneficiary.[32]

We can therefore ascribe the leading political role of the African intelligentsia to the exigencies of the colonial and post-colonial states. The latter's historical priority in Africa, its furtherance of the territorial division and control of African society, has largely determined the predominance and priority of the professional stratum, and delivered into its hands the armoury of bureaucratic control. And here, then, we have the first, *structural*, ground for the leading role of the intelligentsia in Africa today, namely its relationship with the institutions of state.

But that is only one part of the story. There is a second basis for the contemporary predominance of the intelligentsia in the new African states, and that a *cultural* ground, namely, their interdependence with recent ideologies, notably nationalist ones.

The origins of that interdependence are, once again, colonial. Colonial rule bred an ideology of white, Western supremacy, which, openly or subtly, deprecated indigenous

cultures and societies, and tended to classify individuals upon
an ethnic or colour basis (rather than a linguistic one), once the
introduction of Christianity on a large scale removed the
division between believers and heathen.[33] In other words,
cultural distinctions, usually invidious, had by the late 19th
century replaced religious divisions, except perhaps in Islamic
strongholds.[34] Generally speaking, all Africans, being dark-
skinned, were regarded as inferior and in need of 'civilisation';
in the colonial mind, the colour line was all-important (though
not universally, as we saw) and they regarded it as quite natural
that a white-skinned division of humanity should act as rulers,
and a dark-skinned one should be their subjects, in each and
every colonial territory.[35] But, within this overall classification by colour, there also existed more elaborate, if hardly
more subtle, distinctions: those of ethnicity and culture, some
African ethnic communities or 'tribes', as they were dubbed,
being deemed suitable for colonial purposes, notably those of
war, and thought of as the 'martial races' — Berbers, Kurds,
Zulu, Gurkhas — while others like the Kikuyu were spurned
and relegated in the security consciousness of their rulers.[36]
Ethnicity, therefore, was already a classificatory tool in the
colonial era; and it was a favourite charge of later radical
nationalists like Cabral that colonialism, if it did not actually
'invent ethnicity', turned it into a political issue.[37]

Now it was partly to counter this cultural depreciation, as
well as for the economic and political causes that we examined,
that African intelligentsia embraced a 'territorial' mode of
nationalism, which aimed to take over the colonial state and
create a genuine cultural and political community, a 'nation'.
As we also saw, they were partly driven to adopt this policy by
the restrictions placed upon entry into the higher echelons of
the colonial administrations, armies, judiciaries and police
services. This closure was in part 'structural': that is to say, it
was determined, to some degree, by the number of posts in
these institutions available to qualified Africans, and the corresponding number of educated and suitably trained Africans
in each territory. But, within these limitations, racial and
cultural prejudice played a fairly large part in restricting the
number of recruits to central colonial services; in colonial eyes,
there could be no question of the ability of Africans to deter-

mine policy at the higher levels, and hence to be admitted to senior posts in the army or civil service, until, that is, almost the end of the colonial era. Hence, it comes as no surprise to see African nationalists becoming fervently panAfricanist in their ideals, and thereby seeking to nullify the cultural and psychological effects of colonial prejudice and discrimination.[38] Small wonder, too, that in the French territories, above all, where French administrators had laboured to mould the minds of their young African elite charges in the exalted sentiments and glorious history of France and its preeminent Gallic culture, African intellectuals should react vigorously against the neglect or worse of their own cultures, and seek to reinstate those cultures in the minds and hearts of a culturally alienated and displaced intelligentsia.[39] The cult of Négritude which swept West African intellectuals from French-speaking territories, especially those in 'exile' in Paris in the 1950s, reflected these angry but ambivalent feelings, and led to a heightened appreciation of African history, African communities, and the African personality, in sharp contradistinction to the technologically superior but spiritually inferior civilisation of the West.[40] Here, too, was another potent source of African territorial nationalism and its policies of bureaucratic and educational Africanisation, directed especially against expatriate whites and settler or Asian communities in Africa. Nor should we wonder at the collectivistic tone of much African thought of this period, especially as one vital aim of African nationalism was the creation of more bureaucratic posts for Africans, and a replication of bureaucracies, especially in the economic sphere, itself undergoing a rapid process of nationalisation.[41]

But, if the intelligentsia were active in the 'territorial' nationalism of the 1950s, reacting as they did to colonial racial and colour classifications, they also began to come forward as spokesmen and leaders of their respective ethnic communities within the newly independent African states. For, developing *pari passu* with a wider territorial nationalism, there gradually arose more specific movements on behalf of those communities, the 'ethnic nationalisms' which we discussed in the last chapter. Here, too, it was colonial classifications that helped to spur burgeoning ethnic consciousness into political activity and to mobilise their intelligentsia on behalf of the newly urbanised communities.⁴² As the post-colonial state inherited these classifications, and began to allocate resources and posts on an ethnic basis, usually reserving for the dominant and strategically located ethnic community the lion's share, the new ethnic elites soon reacted in the same manner and style as the wider intelligentsia throughout the colonial territory had already done, or was doing. History immediately repeated itself, with the ethnic intelligentsia following the state-wide one hard on its heels; in Nigeria, a territory-wide intelligentsia sought to achieve self-government for all Nigerians and senior political and administrative posts for themselves, only to be swiftly followed by the Ibo intelligentsia in respect of the administration and armed services of the Eastern region.⁴³ It was the intelligentsia who led repeated and successive waves of ethnic unrest, formulating an ethnic nationalism much like that of pan-Africanist 'territorial' nationalism, except that its communal base is smaller and more compact and culturally more homogeneous. Indeed, just as that earlier 'territorial' nationalism mirrored in reverse the features of colonialist perspectives on Africa, so later 'ethnic' nationalisms mirror likewise those entertained by territorial nationalists of each component ethnic community, and react accordingly. Ethnicity, then, has become a major line of cleavage within the ruling stratum itself, and a great source of trouble and worry for the political intelligentsia which finds itself in control of the post-colonial state.⁴⁴

It follows from all this that the main carriers of nationalist ideologies, both territorial and ethnic, are the intelligentsia. Or, more precisely, intellectuals and intelligentsia; those who formulate, analyse and criticise ideas, while taking up any occupation, and those use their higher educational diplomas to engage in vocational activity for a livelihood; those who engage in intellectual activity freely, being interested in rationalism as a mode of critical discourse and in knowledge as a fund of facts and ideas for their own sake, and those who disseminate and apply that knowledge and those ideas, using other people's paradigms for practical and specialist ends: in a word, the dilettante man of ideas, and the professional expert.⁴⁵ Now, by and large, what we generally call 'cultural

nationalism' has been the province of the intellectual, the man
of ideas for ideas' sake, the ideologue.[46] Though cultural
nationalism has been made to appeal to a far wider constituency, including teachers and other 'liberal professions', it
has always constituted the creation and special zone of intellectuals. For they, above all, feel the need for a resolution of
those crises of identity which menace modern man, and which
require of him a moral regeneration, a rediscovery and realisation of self, through a return to that which is unique to oneself,
to one's special character and history, which cannot be severed
from the individuality and unique history of one's own
community.[47] This drive for moral purification and regeneration of the self within a purified and renewed community,
which is the core of cultural nationalism, links the concept of
the ideal 'nation' very closely to the aspirations and activities of
intellectuals in the modern, secular age. For what Weber
termed the 'ideal interests' of intellectuals find a natural outlet
in missionary activity for the national ideal; and, as he remarked, it is intellectuals who are the preeminent bearers of
that ideal.[48] In every country, cultural nationalism which tends
to precede other forms of nationalism, is promulgated
through the literary and educational activities of these intellectuals; each and every renewal of that nationalism owes its
inspiration, in the first place, to intellectuals and their missionary zeal on behalf of the rejuvenated nation.[49]

On the other hand, political nationalism, though it must use
elements drawn from cultural nationalism with its heightening and idealising of national consciousness, focusses on more
immediate and practical issues. Its prime goal is the attainment
of autonomy and self-government for the community, and
the achievement of social cohesion and unity, where these are
neglected or lacking. That usually requires the formation of an
ideological movement bent on unification or secession of the
community, and its attainment of statehood. More pro-
foundly, the essence of political nationalism is fundamentally
civic: the political nationalist wants to communicate a sense of
civic pride, to form an educated and nationally conscious
public and create institutions which will undergird the new
political community or civic nation which is 'struggling for
freedom' and must be 'realised'.[50] Now, this cult of the civic

nation and of public solidarity is close to the heart of the professional. His interests, material and ideal, are closely tied to the creation of a territorial community, based firmly on a recognised homeland in which he may safely and freely practise his specialism, and to the formation of an educated and unified citizenry, which will appreciate and value his specialist skills and his sense of professionalism. Expertise is a valuable commodity only within a competitive and territorially demarcated body of educated citizens, in a world of analogous bodies. It is the more valuable in a community run by bureaucratic institutions in the spheres of government, the economy and the professions, in which a man's occupation determines his standing, and in which knowledge and skill determine a man's occupation. Political nationalism, therefore, the formation of territorially demarcated and socially solidary citizenries within their respective bureaucratic states, is the special province and creation of the professional intelligentsia.

But, if we may say that intellectuals and intelligentsia constitute the carriers of these two types of nationalism, the cultural and the political, it is equally true that the ideology of nationalism, once in being, may be said to 'carry' the intellectuals and intelligentsia, indeed to thrust them forward and upward, to positions of leadership in the community they aim to represent and on whose behalf they do battle. Not that most of them are unwilling 'philosopher-kings'. But that is not the point. The ideology of nationalism has a momentum of its own, once it has been generated in a given area, and once it finds 'bearer' groups within a society.[51] Its particular force resides in its generalising and inclusive character; at once anticolonialist and communitarian, it soon becomes a territory-wide and multi-class ideal, so that those in command of the educational sector, as the intelligentsia inevitably are, find that their adherence to nationalist ideals propels them into the role of organising the motley and heterogeneous coalition of strata and communities that make up the 'nation-to-be', in accordance with those generalist criteria.[52]

In this sense, then, the interdependence of nationalist ideologies and the intelligentsia (and intellectuals) entails a prominent political role for the latter and a strategic position within the new state which they seek to use on behalf of the nascent community. Nationalism has everywhere become the chief ideological vehicle by means of which the intelligentsia is able to stake its claims to leadership, and which helps to rally other strata, including the lowest classes, to their banner. With this ideology strapped to their flag, the intelligentsia emerge as national leaders, and inevitable successors and heirs of colonialism. For they alone of all the groups that make up the new states of post-colonial Africa, can make any claim to act on behalf of the whole community, and to lead an 'African people' duly constituted as a nation-state.

These, then, are the twin routes through which African intelligentsia today have achieved the leading political positions. On the one hand, they have climbed to power through their close and intimate relationships with the colonial and post-colonial states, as a product and beneficiary of their peculiar institutions, and have therefore reaped the reward of their structural position, their social niche. On the other hand, they have been 'borne' upward, as it were, through their strong attachments to certain ideals; their cultural roles and interests have brought them, through the ideology of nationalism, into the leading positions in the community they seek to liberate and support. As we shall see, that leading position is in no way diminished when they embrace, in conjunction, that other ideology of communism.

6 Populism and Communism

Of the ideals that currently motivate African and Asian intelligentsia, two are pre-eminent and near-universal: the drive for development and the quest for national dignity. The relative weight given to development and dignity, and the kinds of strategy for their attainment, vary considerably between the new states at different times, and it is often hard to disentangle their practical aspects. But strategies and goals are more amenable to analytic classification, and we can usefully distinguish three main types of political strategy. The first is individualistic, and it resembles the liberal type of nationalism familiar in Western history, with its emphasis upon laissez-faire competition within an overall territorial framework, on the rights of organised opposition within the national community, and some protection for minorities and civil liberties, within a rational and voluntaristic association.[1] Several Asian and African states like Malaysia, India and Kenya, have gravitated towards this individualistic and rationalist mode of political action. But, generally speaking, this kind of strategy has proved unattractive for most intelligentsia in the new states. They have preferred the other two types, the *étatiste* and the collectivist, the one military and bureaucratic in style and content, the other political and mass-mobilising.[2] It is with the latter strategy that I shall chiefly be concerned, as it throws a great deal of light on the main object of our enquiry, the nature of the political community or 'nation' which Africans and Asians desire to forge.

Not all collectivist strategies share the same assumptions. It may, in fact, be useful to subdivide them into broadly 'social-democratic' and 'marxist' categories, though such Eurocentric labels fail to do justice to the peculiar characteristics of collectivist nationalisms outside Europe. The number of 'pure' marxist regimes in the 'Third World' has been relatively few: China, Vietnam, Kampuchea, South Yemen, Angola, Mozambique, Guinea-Bissau and perhaps Ethiopia and

Somalia, with Cuba and Allende's Chile in southern America. In addition, a number of regimes describe themselves as 'socialist' in a looser sense; they include Burma, Sri Lanka, India, Iraq, Syria, Egypt under Nasser, Algeria, Ghana under Nkrumah, Mali under Keita, Guinea and Tanzania. The distinction between the two varieties of mass-mobilising or collectivist regime in Africa and Asia is often blurred; and it may well be that their similarities are more important than any doctrinal differences.

Indeed, one may be forgiven for hesitating to accept terms like 'socialist nationalism', let alone 'marxist nationalism', as authentic descriptions of a particular strategy adopted by several regimes in Africa and Asia, were it not for the very considerable evidence on the ground for just such a combination. The whole idea of a 'marxist nationalism' is all the more difficult to accept in view of the attitudes of the respective ideologies' founders. Rousseau, Herder and Mazzini might be radicals, but they were in no sense communists;[3] as for Marx and Engels, their official position as revolutionary internationalists precluded any attachment to, or interest in, questions of nationality or nationalism.[4]

Or did it? Curiously, the founders of 'scientific socialism' were rather ambivalent on the subject. Of course, we can find plenty of disparaging comments about nationality in the writings of both Marx and Engels; yet there are also passages that reveal a healthy respect for national independence and an 'honourable national spirit', and a not inconsiderable attachment to Germany. One could indeed maintain that, in this respect, Marx and Engels imbibed the conventional wisdom of their time; and that, especially in less guarded moments in their journalism, they betrayed the usual European prejudices, particularly as regards the 'barbaric' and 'stagnant' nations and 'races' of the 'Third World'.[5]

More pertinently, Marx and Engels also bequeathed a certain theoretical legacy to contemporary marxist nationalists. True, neither took the trouble to provide a general theory of nationalism, or even accord the subject its due during that 'springtime of peoples'; but they did lay down some broad principles to guide socialists in the task of evaluating specific kinds of nationalism. At the most general level, a socialist had to differentiate those nationalisms that were likely to hasten the onset of the proletarian revolution, from those likely to impede it. More specifically, the communist must consider certain key factors, the first being the positive relationship between economic progress and national independence. In the *Communist Manifesto*, Marx and Engels assert that bourgeois development will soon diminish national antagonisms; yet they place great weight on the need for 'united action, of the leading civilised countries at least', to emancipate the proletariat.[6] Moreover, the necessary effect of economic development and progress in the leading, civilised countries, is political centralisation in 'one nation, with one government, one code of laws, one national class-interest, one frontier and one customs-tariff'. This emphasis upon the role of the leading countries — the European 'triarchy' of Moses Hess, namely, England, France and Germany[8] — was to form the cornerstone of the marxist evaluation of national contributions to socialism. There was, of course, nothing arbitrary in this choice: England, France and Germany in the 1840s and 1850s seemed to offer the best chances for a successful proletarian revolution, since they displayed, albeit very unevenly, the capitalist conditions for the rise of the proletariat and of socialism, while in other countries of Europe these conditions were as yet barely visible. To Engels, indeed, 'in any country the rule of the bourgeoisie is impossible without national independence', just as later he was to write to Karl Kautsky that 'To get rid of national oppression is the basic condition of all free and healthy development . . . '.[9] Like latterday marxist nationalists, then, Marx and Engels as early as the 1840s regarded national independence and economic development as twin processes, which were closely interdependent and mutually reinforcing, and which were prerequisites for the rise of both the bourgeoisie and the proletariat, and hence of socialism itself.

Flowing from this first consideration was a second, the belief in the virtue of bigness. Large size and scale were, in turn, prerequisites for capitalism. Free trade, protection, a commodity market, industrialisation, a wage-labour force, all required a large-scale territorial and political framework within which to operate. Engels, in particular, laid great emphasis upon the geographical, military and technological foundations of economic development and national markets.[10] In this, he was also influenced by Hegel and his theory of 'historyless peoples'. Thus he alleged that

Peoples which have never had a history of their own, which from the time when they achieved the first, most elementary stage of civilisation already came under foreign sway, or which were *forced* to attain the first stage of civilisation only by means of a foreign yoke, are not viable and will never be able to achieve any kind of independence.[11]

In this he followed Hegel, who divided nations into 'state-building' ones and those deemed incapable of doing so.[12] It greatly coloured Engels', and even Marx's, attitudes to East European peoples, especially the Czechs and South Slavs, who were held to be incapable (on no very convincing historical grounds) of 'state-building' and who were therefore destined to remain as 'residual fragments of peoples', as were also the Gaels, Bretons and Basques.[13] Marx shared this basic belief in state-building and large-scale centralisation, even if he was less influenced by the theory of 'historyless peoples'. Marx was, after all, particularly interested in German unification without which there could be no real development of capitalist forces of production; he did not, on the whole, approve of small national units, or of federalism. It is great nations that command his support on the ground that they alone can 'become a powerful co-efficient of social production'.[14] On the same grounds, Engels supported the restoration of Poland to her ancient borders; and both Marx and Engels were sympathetic to such large nations as Hungarians, Italians and Germans, while inclined to view the claims of Bulgarians, Czechs, Slovenes and Serbs as 'reactionary' because their size did not permit any real development of capitalism, and their agrarian backwardness and Slav culture was an invitation to that bulwark of absolutist reaction, Tsarist Russia, to intervene.[15]

A third principle for assessing the claims of given nationalisms derived from the overall 'instrumental' nature of Marx's and Engels' view of the national question. This was that 'class' rather than 'ethnic' dimensions were to be sought and preferred in any specific instance, even if it was clear that cultural considerations were as much a motivating factor in a movement as economic ones. For Marx and Engels, nationalism is a purely practical issue. It does not merit a special theory. While the 'nation-state', the great nation of the West, is an inevitable component of social progress during the modern capitalist era, national*ism* and national sentiment, particularly where it appears to conflict with proximate large-scale states, must be discouraged; but it requires no explanation as a phenomenon in its own right. It is simply a complicating factor, one of many that may impede or, more rarely, facilitate the growth of capitalism and later socialism; just as the countries of Africa and Asia may influence, in their turn, the much more advanced development of Europe.[16] What this means is, once again, that the 'great nation-state' of western Europe provides the primary criterion for social progress and its evaluation in every other area; and secondly, that the separate force of the drive for national independence and identity is never acknowledged by the founders of 'scientific socialism'. No doubt, to do so, to have conceded the force of ethnic ties and national sentiments, would have required a very considerable emendation of the whole marxist theory, with its primary emphasis upon socioeconomic rather than cultural determinants and factors in historical development.

The central omission, then, of subsequent marxist theory in this field derived from the founders' failure to grasp the force and nature of ethnic ties, a curious failure for such historically-minded, even historicist, theorists. Perhaps, in advancing a very specific, and special, view of the historical process, one which deliberately underrated cultural dimensions, they could not afford to incorporate a set of characteristics and factors that would have undermined the purity of their conception. It was this defective legacy, at any rate, that subsequent marxists have had to correct and amend.

Eastern European marxists could not afford to overlook the nationalist challenge. They might, like Rosa Luxemburg, try to devalue its significance by suggesting that it was largely confined to the intelligentsia in Poland.[17] More often, however, they conceded its prime importance, and recommended strategies for incorporating the nationality question within an overall socialist revolutionary perspective. Lenin and Stalin, certainly, had a much greater understanding of the vitality of ethnic ties and national passions than their western forebears. In

Russia and eastern Europe, there was hardly any way in which the issue could be glossed over, especially in the years leading up to the Great War. Hence, without abandoning the central marxist tenet that class interests overrode all other forces as the motor of historical progress, Lenin added that it was a socialist duty to fight for the liberation of the nationalities from Tsarist or Habsburg oppression, and that national self-determination was a necessary prelude to socialist revolution in reactionary, feudal empires.[18] Similarly, when he came to consider the plight of Asian peoples, Lenin extended marxist analysis in a way which to some extent undermined Marx's own insistence on the essentially beneficial effects of western imperialism and colonialism; for Lenin, 'imperialism' was essentially an economic phenomenon, an outgrowth and manifestation of mature 'finance capitalism', and hence true socialists must support the just struggle for 'national liberation' waged by the oppressed masses of Asia, in the same way that they supported the workers' struggles within advanced capitalist countries.[19] And yet, for all these strategic advances on Marx's own positions, the Bolsheviks made no real study of the origins and nature of nationalist ties beyond some vague generalities linking them to the rise of capitalism; nor did their attitude to nationalism go beyond the purely instrumental approach of Marx and Engels. Even Lenin's celebrated support for the principle of national self-determination turns out to be largely theoretical and strategic in intent; the right to self-determination is carefully circumscribed by the 'need' or wisdom of secession, in practice. Even his voluble support for anti-colonial nationalism is carefully incorporated within his analysis of socialist advance.[20]

Perhaps only the Austro-marxists, Renner and Bauer, evinced any emotional grasp and psychological and historical understanding of ethnic ties and nationalist ideas. But theirs was a minority stance, repudiated by most marxists in the West as well as the East.[21] In practice, marxists have come ill-equipped, theoretically and emotionally, to the issues raised by the power of national sentiments and ideologies; in both their theory and their practice, they have hewed close to the spirit of the founding fathers, and have retained their central concern for the primacy of the large-scale state over the small-scale communal nation, a concern that combines strength with inflexibility.

Far from being a passing phenomenon of early or late capitalism, nationalism has, in fact, shown remarkable staying power and vigour in all kinds of social settings. Marxists have had to come to terms with continual national eruptions, which show few signs of abating; and, to their credit, they have managed to evolve a *modus vivendi*, sometimes even a close working relationship, with nationalism. Indeed, in several countries a 'marxist nationalism' has become the favoured strategy of development on the part of a section of the intelligentsia, and the official national ideology in such states as Ethiopia, Angola, Mozambique, Guinea–Bissau, Somalia, South Yemen, China, Vietnam, Cambodia and Cuba, not to mention the countries of eastern Europe and Yugoslavia. In several other countries, a vaguer social–democratic 'socialism' is practised; they include Algeria, Guinea, Mali, Syria, Tanzania, Nicaragua and Burma, with several more countries having communist or socialist parties. Why has the communist, or more broadly, the socialist strategy become so attractive a variant of nationalism? Why are we witnessing this 'symbiosis' of communism and nationalism, despite their mutual suspicions and antipathies? What can it offer that other ideologies of the intelligentsia fail to provide?

There are, I think, three main reasons why the marxist-nationalist variant has emerged as a vital force in under-developed countries in the last four decades: ideological, sociological and geopolitical. The ideological parallelism permits a symboiosis; the sociological situation of the intelligentsia propels them towards it; while the international situation provokes them into it.

Having dealt at greater length elsewhere with the question, I shall be brief with the ideological parallels between communism and nationalism[22] The main point is that, as belief-systems, they possess similar formal structures and enough parallels in imagery to permit a genuine symbiosis, in certain circumstances. Basically speaking, they both present a tripartite historicist vision of humanity's progress: a present state of oppression, a period of transition and transcendence, and a vision of the messianic future. In addition, both possess images of a golden past, albeit rude and simple, whose virtuous characteristics must somehow be incorporated into the golden future. To spell this out briefly: the world as we find it, is in a sad state of oppression and distortion. It is locked into an alienating system of tyranny and deracination. For the marxist, the oppressor is the capitalist class, the bourgeoisie, and the system is commodity capitalism. For the nationalist, the oppressor is the alien nation, and the system is corrupting cosmopolitanism. For the marxist, the result is alienation of the proletariat, the turning of human beings into labour power for sale on the commodity market. For the nationalist, the result is estrangement and homelessness, the turning of rooted men and women into exiles and refugees and second-class citizens in their own countries. How can we transcend this oppressive condition? Through a mixture of evolution and revolution, of progress with force. For marxism, capitalism will be superseded only when the material conditions for its transcendence have matured within the 'womb' of capitalism itself; but the act of transcending the old state is never mechanical, it requires human understanding and participation; political revolution must supplement social evolution.[23] For nationalism, the nation will gradually 'awaken' from its lack of self-consciousness and when its members have realised themselves as members of that nation, the time for liberation will be at hand; then gradualism will cede place to struggle, a struggle for men's minds through the weapon of education, and for men's bodies through the use of force against the alien oppressors. The growth of the nation to full self-consciousness and true identity requires active participation in a holy war of liberation.[24] And what, finally, will this struggle and transcendence achieve? A true relation of man to the community. In place of the old false egoism and fragmentation, man will realise his true social nature and identity. The communist sees this true state emerging with the re-integration of man with society, he sees the humanisation of man as his socialisation, and the restoration of man to himself through the community.[25] The nationalist sees the true state as one in which the nation has become a regenerated community, a genuine fraternity because it has rediscovered its origins and rootedness, and thereby its fundamental identity and destiny.

Through this rediscovery, man too can find his identity and purpose in life; for his 'essence', his reality, if you like, can only be realised in and through his regenerated community, which defines his being and individuality. And for communists and nationalists, the true state, which is really a dynamic process of becoming, has been prefigured in the past, when man was 'pure' and undistorted, but undeveloped and unrealised, a primordial being without individuality, without history, without complexity.

These are some of the formal structures and parallelisms that allow marxists and nationalists to blur their ideological differences, to fuse their imagery, and to assimilate each other's perspectives. A long line of 'marxist-nationalists' — Mao, Tito, Ho Chi Minh, Castro, Neto, Machel and Cabral — and an even greater number of socialistic nationalists — Nasser, Ben Bella, Aflaq, Nkrumah, Sekou Toure, Sukarno, Nyerere, Nehru and U Nu — have managed to identify the common images and themes of the two traditions and adapt both to the specific local conditions and political situations in which they found themselves. They have, for example, often fused the class struggle of the workers with the 'people's struggle' of the nation against foreign oppressors, as the Chinese communists did in the late 1930s after the Japanese invasion.[26] They have identified the struggle against the bourgeoisie and the nationalisation of bourgeois property with the war against 'imperialism', and western interests and holdings.[27] They have been adept at amalgamating the state-based nationalism of the colonial territory with the Party-State, the state controlled by a single party, and at identifying the 'nation' itself with the 'people', usually the peasant masses whom the Party wished to mobilise.[28] In all these ways, marxist nationalists have fused the two separate traditions, both at the theoretical and the practical levels.

More important, for our purposes, are the social conditions that have impelled this fusion. Communist nationalisms tend to emerge in small circles of the urban intelligentsia, often formed into semi-secret societies or cells and excluded from any participation in politics, if not actually persecuted. Colonial regimes, of course, had no place for such sects, but the latter have often fallen foul of their nationalist successors, whether single-party regimes or local military overlords like Chiang Kai-Shek or Batista, whose radicalism and national credentials have been lost or become suspect. Two situations commonly provide fertile soil for the emergence and success of socialist or communist nationalisms: where a colonial power hangs on to its possessions well beyond the time when the world situation permitted it, or where they sought to regain those possessions; thus the Portuguese hung on in Angola, Mozambique and Guinea-Bissau, and the French in Algeria, and the French sought to regain Indo-China and the Dutch Indonesia. The second situation occurs where a local sovereign state has a weak or inefficient or personalistic government, riddled with corruption, as was the case with Batista and Somoza or the Kuomintang and the Wafd in Egypt, all of whom moreover depended upon a foreign power or powers to keep them in office; in this case, too, the communists are offended by social inequities and corruption, while the nationalists are disenchanted by the foreign entanglements and dependence. In all these examples the existing regime is held guilty on two counts: failing to provide strong and effective government, which can 'stand on its own feet' without being beholden to some distant great power, and failing to mobilise the people for the development that has been delayed so long and which intensifies political dependence through stagnation and backwardness. Once again, the ideals of development and national dignity are inextricably interwoven, and both have been trampled on.

In fact, just these were the typical situations that obtained in Africa. In Ethiopia, for example, the military officers who engineered the coup that ousted the royal family and the aristocracy, were initially driven by their impotent fury at the government's failure to palliate the effects of the terrible drought and famine of 1974, and later by the country's dependence on the economic and political (and military) power of the United States. Delayed development, interpreted as a by-product of ossified feudalism, was mingled with corrupt and ineffective government in the minds of the young radicals, and both in turn were traced to an excessive dependence upon a foreign power who could dictate internal as well as external policy. It was a foreign power who ensured the survival of the feudal nobility in large parts of the Ethiopian empire, the domination of the Amhara and the relative failure to modernise rapidly enough. And yet, by a typical paradox, such partial modernisation as Haile Selassie had begun, had thrown up a small educated stratum on whom he increasingly depended, especially in staffing his expanded army; and it was from this isolated sector, that the movement to topple his regime and give Ethiopia a modern economy and social structure was initiated. The intelligentsia–in–arms, in the absence of a large civilian stratum of professionals, take over the state and direction of policy and develop a populist, and later a communist, critique of society and government.[29]

In the Portuguese territories, the oppressor was in any case a foreign, European power, which made few pretensions of developing its African possessions, and was itself ruled by a dictatorship at home. Here, the very length of possession, and the stagnant nature of its hold, contributed to the growth of a socialist, and then a marxist, critique of colonialism and society. Again, it was a very small stratum of intelligentsia that were actively involved in the guerilla war. They had originated as a political opposition in the towns; in Angola, they divided along ethnic lines, and only one of the guerilla groups managed to evolve a fully marxist line.[30] In all the cases, they moved to the bush, and fought a popular war of liberation, appealing to the peasant masses and mobilising them for help and shelter and flight, as Mao had recommended and Guevara practised it. In each case, the movement turns first 'populist'; that is to say, it adopts the ideals of popular participation by the peasantry, of economic autarchy through self–help, and of agricultural development through local rural institutions.[31] Its critique of government gradually focusses on economic issues of land reform and rural development; to counter national dependance and dishonour, it must mobilise the mass of the population, utilise their energies, turn them into active citizens. Only through a strong social and economic base in the countryside can the nation become regenerated and corruption and dependence be overcome.[32]

It is important to distinguish this form of urban 'populism' from the rural versions practised by small farmers or the popular peasant uprisings in the countryside, the jacqueries that have occurred throughout history, and which so often failed for lack of urban leadership and a clear ideology.[33] The main point about the populism that forms the matrix of communist nationalisms is that it is a strictly urban phenomenon of the secular intelligentsia and serves their material interests and cultural needs, rather than those of the peasants it aims to support. Many members of this urban intelligentsia come from the petty-bourgeois stratum; as sons of small traders, shopkeepers, clerks and artisans, they retain the values of the 'small man' in his struggles against big organisations, large corporations or unions or government, and are attracted by the sort of urban populism which is deeply suspicious of the new order of large bureaucratic organisations.[34] Many also idealise the past and the apparent stability of its hierarchical order and rural environment. Of course, the professional intelligentsia has broken with that past. Its material interests are firmly rooted in the new bureaucratic order and its skills and attitudes only possess meaning within a 'modernist' framework. And yet, because of the social origins of some of its members (not all the intelligentsia come from the artisan or shopkeeper stratum), and because its route to prominence has taken it outside the usual avenues to wealth and power in large-scale business or governmental organisations, the professional stratum feels also estranged from the new order. A populist critique of modern society offers them a programme in which their social isolation and political powerlessness can be overcome. By adopting the vague socioeconomic analysis of populism, by linking their own fate to that of the 'small man' in the city and the peasant masses outside, by 'going to the people', the intelligentsia can find a social base for its rise to political power and an economic outlet for their professional services.

Moreover, urban populism answers many of the cultural needs and perplexities of the newly educated strata. Their isolation is as much cultural as social. They are caught between nostalgia for a disintegrating social order and its traditional values, and the attractions and promises of western culture with its rationalist mode of discourse. Although products of the latter culture, they yearn for reintegration into the old, indigenous framework with its hallowed customs and unique meanings. Or rather they long for the warmth and security, as they imagine it, of the old ways, but without its impositions, its hierarchies and its obscurantism. Exactly this ambivalence and tension provides fertile soil for nationalism and populism. Nationalism furnishes an overall image of the world, divided into historic culture-communities seeking political recognition. Populism interprets the culture-bearing community as a popular, democratic organism, its culture expressing the folkways of the small man and the peasant which have evolved over centuries and have stamped the community with their distinctive character. Populism, in this urban sense, becomes a phase or moment of nationalism, one of its many interpretations, but one which answers to the cultural needs of intelligentsia in less developed societies overshadowed by the scientific and political preeminence of the West. For populism offers a means of 're-rooting' an estranged and deracinated professional stratum, back into the community from which their critical culture and rationalist education has so insidiously parted them. In this way, a romantic nationalism slides towards an urban populism that extols rural folkways.[35]

But inchoate yearnings and nostalgic aspirations must be translated into political action. Here, communism has much to offer a populist professional. For the urban intellectual is likely to lack both a strategy and a vehicle for harnessing the potential of the urban and rural masses he aims to mobilise against the local or foreign ruling strata. Classic marxism offers both: a strategy that can give direction to populist aspirations, and a means of realising that strategy through concerted action. Through the concepts of imperialism and social revolution, and the vehicle of the Party-movement and Party-state, classical marxism can channel and direct the intelligentsia's populism towards clearcut political goals of the sort that populism, by itself, often lacks. Conversely, communism finds in the intelligentsia's populistic nationalism fertile soil for the propagation of its special reading of history and its unique vision of the future. Typically, a few intellectuals and ex-students in underdeveloped countries, often from the bourgeois or petty-bourgeois strata, take the vague socio-economic critique of populism and social-democracy much further, underpinning it with a revised version of western marxism. To fit the very different conditions of underdeveloped countries, the communist intellectuals must select some central themes from classical marxism, relegate others, and add still others to the canon. From marxism itself, they tend to retain, first, an identification with the exploited classes; but, in this case, their intepretation is rather broader than Marx's own identification of the proletariat as the 'universal class' of Hegelian theory.[36] For Mao and Ho Chi Minh, the toiling masses included that class which constitutes the great bulk of the population in agrarian countries, the peasantry; and to the peasants, indeed, most guerilla movements of communist nationalism have been forced to appeal. Tito, Mao, Castro, Che Guevara, Ho Ch Minh, Ben Bella, Cabral, Neto, Machel are among the many socialist and communist nationalists who have been compelled by force of circumstances to modify an urban theory and wage guerilla 'peasant wars' to mobilise the countryside against the urban centres controlled by the exploiting classes.[37] Second, communist nationalism has extracted from the marxist corpus its commitment to social revolution against the oppressor classes, if necessary a violent revolution, so as to remove all obstacles to the path of socialist development; but again, they have re-interpreted those obstacles and that class more broadly, to cover the capitalist forces of 'imperialism' who underpin native ruling classes, as the United States companies shored up the Batista regime in Cuba during the 1950s.[38] In other cases, the colonial power itself was identified with the capitalist ruling class, as in the Portuguese territories. Hence the first task was to eliminate the foreign presence which distorted and fragmented the nation, and then go on to mobilise the masses, nationalise private property, Africanise all posts and sectors, and embark on a crash programme of massive industrialisation, as the sole route to both national dignity and a socialist community.[39] Social revolution was therefore necessary, not just to surpass capitalism, but also to overcome imperialism and realise the fraternity of a truly national community.

As a concomitant of these modifications of classical marxism, communist nationalisms have tended to reinterpret 'class conflict', that central premise of the marxist conception of history, in the light of Lenin's theory of imperialism. They have tended to stress the 'organic' nature of underdeveloped societies and laid most of the blame for any internal oppression on small circles of wealthy capitalists or feudal traditionalists in league with foreign colonial powers or capitalist multi-nationals. In other words, they accepted Marx's contention that 'class conflict' was the motor of historical development, but transposed it on to the world stage, identifying whole nations as 'proletarian' in the dialectic of world history, and others as 'bourgeois'. Tiny circles of local feudal or capitalist 'collaborators' could then be easily dismissed as tools of imperialism, and the nation remain pure. From the standpoint of nationalism, marxist interpretations simply added another means of identifying the national enemy and his internal collaborators.

By transposing class conflict on to the inter-state level, communist nationalism also prepared the way for the third element selected from the classical European canon; but this time, they have drawn on Lenin's heritage rather than Marx's. In order to mobilise the peasant and urban masses and indus-trialise rapidly, communist nationalism has been forced to look to Lenin's model of the Party of professional revolu-tionaries acting as the vanguard of the oppressed class or nation. A strong Party-based movement, with strict central control and a tight command structure, was found to be essential for conducting prolonged guerilla warfare against the armed superiority of colonialism and its allies, as Guevara and Debray argued in Latin America.[40] It was also indispensable if peasant masses were to be incorporated and mobilised within a politically-directed military organisation. As Huntington has argued, the Leninist model of the Party has proved valuable both in the struggle for independence and in the running of the State after its attainment.[41] In a sense, the cadres and institu-tions built up during the phase of guerilla warfare set the pattern for the informal networks of organisation which will take over and redirect the formal organs of the bureaucratic State which the movement aims to conquer. They form, as it were, a state within the State, a 'counter-state' which must then be reintegrated with the formal State apparatus and take over its direction. A task that is made all the more necessary by the ideological need for political control over the economy and the communist goal of restructuring the nation towards socialist development. In aiming, therefore, to wrest the State apparatus from the control of the colonial powers and their collaborators, communist nationalists necessarily underwrite the need for, and efficacy of, the territorial State. By seeking their main social base among the peasantry outside the cities, by adopting programmes of land reform along with industrialisation, the communist nationalists demonstrate their impatience with ethnic or regional divisions within the colony; for they aim, through their Party institutions, to incorporate the peasant masses everywhere and strip them of their local attachments and cultural traditions, especially where these impede their social and political goals. To have courted the urban proletariat alone, would have exposed the communist nationalists to sure defeat, political as well as military; the cities, after all, were the bulwark of the colonial or ex-colonial order, the proletariat was in its infancy, and the only way to counter the challenge of the State was through the formation of a parallel state based upon the rural masses out of reach of the colonial authorities, but always with the aim of returning to substitute their own political creations for those of colonialism.

The main effects of the communist version of nationalism, and the main reason for its success over even populism, are twofold. On the one hand, the impact of communist nationalism is strongly to reinforce the claims of the territorial state and to legitimate its authority and the integrity of its boundaries. This facet of marxist nationalism is clearly to the fore in Ethiopia, where the regime of Mengistu, as of his Bolshevik models, is bent on retaining the whole territory of the Ethiopian empire intact in the face of various attempts at secession, notably in Eritrea and the Ogaden. In this respect, marxist nationalism cannot tolerate *political* diversity, though it may accord its minorities a measure of cultural pluralism.[42] In Angola the attempts of the marxist-nationalist government to impose its own scheme of things while preserving the territorial integrity of the ex-colony has been so far even less successful, despite Cuban aid. But, as with Mozambique, Algeria and other African countries where socialist experiments and communist programmes have been implemented, there has never been any doubt about the political direction of communist nationalisms. In line with Marx's ideas about the need for 'great nation-states', and Engels' beliefs in militarism and state-building communities, contemporary communist nationalist strategies are founded upon the realisation of political goals within the framework of a strong and preferably large territorial State; for only a large-scale, powerful formation can defend the people's progress towards socialism at the military and political levels, while affording a large enough market for the development of the forces of production, for the accumulation of capital through savings and for the creation of labour-intensive industries able to produce commodities on the world market at competitive prices, a necessary stage in the transition to socialism.[43]

On the other hand, considerable benefits accrue to the intelligentsia which pursues marxist versions of nationalism. By creating a Leninist Party-state, by forming networks of Party institutions and reinforcing the centralising drive of the bureaucratic state, an intelligentsia may have the chance of compensating for its social isolation and cultural cleavages. By politicizing its identity problems and social alienation, by projecting these outward on to the international arena, and seeing in a strong State the active solvent of its own as well as its community's problems, the professional stratum hopes to counteract its own marginal position. Not only does the bureaucratic state offer niches for its professional and organisational skills and talent, which would otherwise be wasted in many underdeveloped societies; it also offers them the best hope for regenerating and reintegrating themselves within a community from which their professional education has cut them off. Moreover, by identifying their own alienation and isolation with the powerlessness of their community, and tracing both to the effects of colonial underdevelopment and imperialist depredations, communist nationalisms provide a theoretical basis for such reintegration and regeneration. No doubt, this helps to explain the appeal of 'dependency theories' within the underdeveloped countries themselves; they function at the practical level more as 'operational' than as purely 'analytical' theories, their prescriptive element revealing the nationalist thrust of their praxis while their theoretical analysis has demonstrated its ability to account for the intelligentsia's situation within its community.[44]

While 'dependency theories' have undoubtedly helped to focus attention on the global context of underdevelopment, they have tended to neglect political and military aspects of the geopolitical situation. But the relations between states and ethnic communities have often provoked the recent symbiosis between communism and nationalism in underdeveloped countries. This has also been the case in Africa, and I want to look briefly at some aspects of this influence.

Perhaps the most obvious dimension has been the catalytic effect of foreign invasion or colonial tenacity. The classic instance of foreign invasion inciting the xenophobic passions of the peasantry to the subsequent advantage of communist nationalists was China in the 1930s. There Mao's rural success came with the effects of the Japanese invasion of 1937, after the Long March and after his earlier land reform populist policies had achieved only a limited success in the southwest of the country.[45] It was the spirit of patriotism with which the communists fought off the Japanese invaders that impressed the peasantry; just as it was the nationalist spirit of Tito's partisans that rallied the Serbian peasants to his cause after 1941, rather than his marxism.[46] In Africa, the situation was rather different. With the exception of the Italian invasion of Ethiopia in the 1930s, which stimulated neither peasant populism nor communist nationalist resistance, there was no foreign invasion to stimulate peasant xenophobia. The communist nationalists had a more difficult task, especially in the Portuguese territories: to instil a spirit of guerilla resistance in the countryside, and in this they were, of course, helped by the repression of colonial government and armies in the villages and tribal areas.[47]

A more pervasive and important geopolitical aspect has been the all-embracing rivalry of the superpowers, one of which was itself committed to the doctrines of marxism, and whose practice displayed an often uneasy mixture of communist and nationalist aims. In a world deliberately divided into competing states (misleadingly called 'nation-states') on the Western model, and after 1945 dominated by superpowers and their client-systems, each replete with competing ideologies and armaments, the possibilities for securing external support from the Soviet Union, or even China, inevitably helped to sharpen the communist elements within local radical or populist nationalisms. Of course, communist influence in Africa slightly antedated this superpower rivalry, having been introduced into West Africa mainly through the French communist party and unions;[48] but it was greatly enhanced by the Soviet practice of support for 'national liberation struggles' recommended by Lenin and his successors. Radical and communist nationalisms have looked for aid and arms to the Soviet Union both in southern Africa and the Horn; so much so, in the latter case, that the Soviet Union has found itself in a dilemma between Somali and Ethiopian claims.[49] The effect of this conjuction of circumstances was to accentuate the anti-Western and revolutionary impulse of nascent communist nationalisms in Angola, Mozambique, Guinea-Bissau, Ethiopia and Somalia, and to some extent in Zimbabwe and Namibia, and to hasten that equation of nation with proletarian class status that forms the central pivot of the communist-nationalist symbiosis.

To view the international context only from the standpoint of local communist-nationalist movements can be misleading, since the rival superpowers and their clients aim to influence the social and ideological complexion of nonaligned areas. Local movements do not only 'suck in' external power rivalries, heightening local tensions; the great powers may seek out openings for intervention and subversion, as in the protracted Arab-Israeli conflict or in southeast Asia. In the Horn, the two processes have gone hand in hand, so that it becomes increasingly difficult to determine cause and effect in the direction of influence between local conflicts and superpower rivalries. In fact, the growing Russian influence in the Somali army in the late 1960s had helped to reorient the regime of General Siyad, after its 1969 coup, towards scientific socialism and with it went a strong denunciation of tribalism, which the official slogan stated 'divides where Socialism unites'.[50] Similarly, Cuban aid in Angola has contributed to the marxist component of the Luanda government; just as, earlier, growing Russian aid to Cuba hastened her progress towards a fully-fledged communist nationalism. The point is that, because the lines of ideological influence within Europe are congealed, great power rivalries naturally seek out a power vacuum in areas of chronic local instability; and, in the Soviet and Chinese cases, the retreat of the European colonialists and the overthrow of traditional regimes offer ideal circumstances for the insertion of communist-nationalist regimes and programmes.

But this great power competition for recruits to the capitalist or communist client-systems operates within certain rules. Broadly speaking, these are the outcome of the structure of states which constitute the world order itself, and which therefore underpin the legitimacy of all states, including the superpowers and their respective clients. In this structure, the 'territorial state' always takes priority over the 'cultural nation', wherever these (and their respective interests) diverge. The Soviet Union itself, like China, forms as much a component of this order of territorial states as the Western powers; indeed, neither communist superpower can make any claims to constituting a 'cultural nation'. In fact, there are very few of these latter in the world today; the world of politics is a world of territorial states rather than cultural nations, and has been created in the image of the original European territorial states, very few of whom are today or were at any time 'cultural nations' as well.[51]

What this means, in practice, is that the scientific socialism practised by the new states or espoused by guerilla movements may only hope to receive Soviet or Chinese aid, if its claims are territorial or it governs a territorial state. Marxist-communism, as practised by the two great communist superpowers, must lend its full weight to the territorial integrity of the state, rather than the secessionist or irredentist claims of the cultural nation. Hence, few ethnic 'liberation struggles' can hope to gain much support from the communist powers; for the latter view ethnic secession with disapproval, even fear. That is one reason why so few ethnic secession movements have succeeded; even where a great power has sometimes viewed their claims with favour, as with the Kurds, Palestinians or Eritreans, this has only occurred where other local states have espoused the secessionist or irredentist cause, as India did with Bangladesh; and only to a very limited degree, even then.

Geopolitical factors, then, have combined with marxist

tradition to underwrite the legitimacy of territorial nationalisms and territorial states, at the expense of ethnicity and
cultural nationalism, with very few exceptions. For these
nationalisms and states form an intrinsic part of the existing
state system which marxist theory and communist practice is
committed to upholding in the interests of socialist revolution.

In recent years, the West has become alarmed at what it
considers to be Soviet penetration of Africa. Its apprehensions,
first aroused by Somalia's turn to the Soviet Union, were to
some extent relieved by Sadat's expulsion of Russian personnel from Egypt; they were revived by the sight of Cuban
soldiers and Russian arms being ferried into Angola to help the
MPLA in their struggle with UNITA, and by Neto's subsequent victory. Their fears were further aggravated by the
rise to power of Colonel Mengistu's faction within the
Ethiopian revolutionary council of the army, his brutal repression of opposition and his break with America and espousal of
marxist nationalism, backed by Soviet support and Cuban
troops, in 1977. Large parts of Africa, it seemed, were already
under communist-nationalist regimes and liable to Soviet
subversion. More recently, however, signs appeared that the
communist tide was ebbing. To begin with, China's cultural
revolution had subsided, and it began to enter into relations
with America and other Western powers. In Somalia, the
regime, angered by Soviet support for Mengistu's regime and
his claims on the Ogaden area, has turned back to Chinese aid
and begun to enter into relations with America. In Mozambique, the Machel government has retreated from its advanced
socialist programme to allow some scope for foreign, and
private, enterprise; while in Guinea-Bissau, there has been a
coup against the Cabral regime. Even in Angola, the MPLA
government has not been able to end the ethnic civil war with
Savimbi's forces; while in Zimbabwe, the much-heralded turn
towards marxist socialism by the Mugabe government has
not, so far, materialised, and relations with the Western
powers have been maintained to meet the costs of the savage
war and of reconstruction.

Undoubtedly, a major shift in the realities and images of the
great powers has contributed to a less favourable ideological
and political climate for socialist experiments in Africa.

American power appears to have declined in the late 1970s, in the aftermath of the Vietnam war and Watergate and a succession of restrained Presidents; while Soviet power was seen to be growing, partly as a function of American contraction, and its intentions were held to be increasingly aggressive. Whatever the truth of these perceptions, they have made many African states more wary of foreign aid and entanglements. Moreover, communist nationalisms, once in power, have had to grapple with intractable problems of development, State power and ethnicity, the selfsame problems that have beset their non-socialist neighbours. Given the dependant nature of African economies and their strongly agrarian basis, the communist commitment to rapid and massive industrialisation without sufficient capital accumulation (and Western refusal to invest) has proved something of a handicap, especially where African leaders have refused to contemplate a Stalinist strategy with its massive human costs, or the complete subordination of their states to external control. They have therefore preferred a more gradual policy of agricultural diversification to avoid dependance on the fluctuations of world commodity markets and reliance on a single primary product. For the same reasons, the overcentralised bureaucratic apparatus of both State and Party in communist regimes, while it ensures the integrity of the post-colonial territory, has proved something of a burden in the task of mobilising local energies for the tasks of modernisation. Its monolithic structure of control may quell regional or ethnic dissidence, but it also fails to instil popular commitment to the regime. Besides, its marxism has become increasingly threadbare, given the leaders' impatience with Marx's time-scale for historical development; political action must pre-empt what economic conditions have failed to secure in a world that cannot wait for African 'maturity'. As for the Leninist legacy of organisation, that too can be absorbed by other, less rigid, forms of nationalism which allow more scope for special African conditions.[52]

But, undoubtedly, the most serious failure of African marxist-nationalisms has been their dismissal of deepseated ethnic divisions as so many relics of 'tribalism' left by the debris of colonialism. Classical marxism, as we saw, had no

theory of ethnic sentiments, and little appreciation of their
vitality and staying-power; it tended to dismiss them as
bourgeois inventions or as vestiges of a 'tradition' that, like
religion, it completely failed to understand. In addition,
marxism, as a strictly urban phenomenon concerned with the
struggle of purely urban classes (the bourgeoisie and the proletariat), was at something of a disadvantage in its competition
with nationalism for the allegiance of the peasant masses. It
had to invoke national sentiment to win them over, and then
turn its back upon them in its drive for industrialisation; while
nationalism can continue to extol the beauty of the countryside, the simplicity of folkways and the virtues of regenerated
peasant masses, in the tradition of Rousseau.[53]

In fact, though it may not care to admit it, communist
nationalisms have tended to succeed either in mono-ethnic
states like Somalia or as the vehicles of one or more specific
ethnic communities, as in Angola and Guinea-Bissau. A
clearcut ethnic base has proved to be all-important for waging
guerilla war and seizing power in the territorial state; but, as in
Yugoslavia during the Second World War, communist
nationalists, though they start from a specific ethnic base,
operate on a territorial plane and present their movement as a
multi-ethnic vehicle of territorial development. And, whatever the ethnic origins of the leaders, communist nationalists
attempt to play down the significance of ethnic ties, even when
strategy requires that they make their appeal to particular
ethnic groups. In practice, however, their chosen ethnic
group(s) remain the fulcrum of the post-independence state,
and its chief beneficiary. In Yugoslavia, the Serbs continue as
the lynchpin of the federation; in Angola that role is taken by
the Akwambundu around Luanda, but their leading role, and
that of the marxist-nationalist government, has not been fully
accepted by the rival movements based upon the other ethnic
communities, the Ovimbundu and the BaKongo, each of
which has thrown up its intelligentsia and guerilla cadres.

To see how marxist nationalists try to cope with the vexing
issues of ethno-nationalism, for which their theory offers little
guidance where it is not positively harmful, we may turn to
Cabral's dilemmas in Guinea-Bissau. Here, in a microcosm,
all the varied facets of the symbiosis and rivalry of com-

munism and nationalism present themselves. Cabral and his family, as well as his chief lieutenants, coming from the Cape Verde islands, and being of mixed Cape Verdean and African descent, were among the *assimilados*, those who had been brought up in Portuguese culture and imbibed it to the full, some of them even studying for their university degrees in Portugal, like Cabral himself. Not only had they received a thoroughly Portuguese education, these Cape Verdeans came from socially advantaged circles, being sons of merchants or bureaucrats.[54] In 1952, Cabral as part of his employment, conducted an agricultural census of Guinea-Bissau; and thereby became extremely well-informed about the mixed ethnic composition of this Portuguese possession. About 90% (or over 500,000) of the population of the territory lived in the countryside at this period. Of these, the largest ethnic group in linguistic and historic terms were the Balanta and other Senegambians, who constituted about 250,000 or nearly half the total rural population. Next came the Fula, some 110,000 strong; then the Manjaco, who numbered 72,000, and last the Mandinga with about 64,000 members. It was to the Balanta and other Senegambian groups that Cabral and his Partido Africano de Independencia da Guine-Bissau e Cabo Verde (PAIGC) made their initial appeal in the long and arduous struggle against Portugal. And it was by exploiting with considerable skill the various interethnic conflicts of which he had learnt so much, that Cabral's movement was able to outstrip its 'bourgeois' rivals. For the territory of Guinea-Bissau had only been fully united by the Portuguese in the 1930s, well after the Fula invasions of the 19th century, which had caused other ethnic communities like the Mandinga much suffering; so Cabral was able to turn old wounds, whose memory was still alive, to his movement's advantage and successfully woo the Mandinga in their strategic territory during the 1960s. Without these ethnic bases, first among the Senegambians, then among the Mandinga, the tiny marxist-nationalist movement would never have got off the ground, or been able to harness and mobilise the peasantry against the Portuguese- and Fula-dominated cities. In all this struggle, despite his territorial, and officially cross-ethnic, appeal, the Fula and their Manjaco allies remained aloof from Cabral and the PAIGC. Nevertheless, by 1974 the Portuguese, with revolution at home, had conceded defeat; and Cabral's PAIGC inherited the colonial legacy of interethnic rivalries.

For Cabral, these ethnic divisions were a dying legacy of Portuguese 'divide-and-rule' policies, and would shortly disappear. The various peoples of Guinea, Cabral declared, were already freeing themselves 'from attitudes of tribal strife', encouraged by colonialism. Cabral himself, like most of his circle, did not belong to any of the main ethnic communities; indeed, they were truly marginal to Guinean society of any kind, and, as Lyon points out,

His understanding of ethnic or national ties as they functioned in Africa was an intellectual one, not emotional. Marxism as a doctrine reinforced, explained and justified such a detached attitude.[55]

With such an 'alien' background, it is hardly surprising if the radical policies of the PAIGC encounter, not merely socioeconomic, but also *ethnic* opposition among the Fula and Manjaco, whom the movement had so signally failed to win over. Small wonder, too, that there has recently been a successful coup against the Cabral-dominated government, although its founder, Amilcar, had already died. Ethnicity has, in this instance, proved stronger than marxism, revealing the essentially nationalist foundations of the liberation struggle, in the hearts and minds of the masses who followed the PAIGC. It was the fact that they alone were prepared to fight the Portuguese, rather than any of their marxist theories or concepts, that inspired so many Senegambians and Mandinga to join them.

And that has been the fate of most of the marxist-nationalist movements, which retain their independence of foreign control to this day. Their nationalism has proved far more effective and significant both for the intelligentsia, and the strata who support them, than their often arid and abstract marxism.

7 Forging Territorial Nations

Central to this account of recent social and political change in Africa and Asia has been the confrontation and interplay of Western ideals and forms with indigenous structures and cultures. We find this interaction, not only in the ideologies and choices of the political leadership and intelligentsia, but more fundamentally in the dominant patterns of national formation in Africa and Asia. On a global scale, we can distinguish four main patterns of national development or formation. The first type, associated with Western Europe, has been marked by continuous conquest and consolidation. In such states as Spain, France, Holland, Britain, Sweden and Russia, what Seton-Watson has called the 'old, continuous nations' have been gradually formed through processes of homogenisation and consolidation by strong territorial dynasties.[1] In the course of this development, absolute monarchs and their ministers had to override strong local opposition and curtail rudimentary forms of democracy, in order to weld their populations and domains together into compact units subject to a uniform body of law and a standardised administrative culture.[2] A second type was, historically, an offshoot of the first. Here, groups of immigrants colonised vast territories already partly inhabited by native societies, which they subjugated; this occurred in Australia and South Africa, Canada and the United States, and here the state was only a part-sponsor of these ventures.[3] Third in historical development came the ethnic pattern typical of central and Eastern Europe, but also to be found in parts of the Middle East. Here the ethnic community formed itself into a politically conscious nation, which then sought to secede from the large-scale empire into which it had been incorporated and set up its own state, and then to unify within the expanded frontiers of that state all those who were felt to belong to the ethnic culture.[4] And finally come the state-based territorialisms, with which we have been mainly concerned in Africa and parts of Asia, and which are the deliberate products of circles formed within earlier patterns of national formation.

Cutting across and complicating these historical patterns has been the ethnic composition of the area in which states were being built up. This has ranged from areas in which the ethnic culture was fairly homogeneous to others where it has been markedly heterogeneous. That is to say, there have been areas where it was possible to form states on the basis of a culturally homogeneous population, as in Portugal, Denmark (with the exception of the Faroese) and, today, Poland and Hungary; and others, where the populations are so intermingled, that the resulting state has been necessarily poly-ethnic. In fact, very few states today are mono-ethnic, in the strict sense of that term. Most contain small minorities of cultural aliens, while many have quite large communities possessing a different culture, as in Canada, Belgium or Czechoslavakia. These are, in fact, 'bi-ethnic' states; others like Switzerland, Yugoslavia, India and Nigeria are poly-ethnic. And it is this latter type of ethnic composition which characterises most African states, and several Asian ones, too.

To grasp the implications of this for political change in those continents, we need to turn back to the peculiar Western pattern of conquest and consolidation, first within Europe and then outside. This Western pattern has been unique in several respects. For one thing it set the framework and provided models for all subsequent patterns, however much the latter diverged from them. For another it was a continuous and largely internal development, even it if was not completely spontaneous. It lacked the planned and premeditated character of later patterns, developing, as it did, over centuries rather than decades. And finally, it was both ethnic and territorial, almost simultaneously. At each step, the 'nation' was being formed within the 'state'; each advance in state-making produced an equivalent step towards nation-formation. National identities were formed in and around the dynastic state, which moulded those identities in its own image, at the cost of cultural minorities within the state.[5]

Today's ethnic composition within the Western states tends to reflect this historical development. Taking place, as it did, in a pre-democratic era, by force of arms, it has tended to create a special kind of plural state, one in which a large ethnic community forms the core of the state and, overtly or not, dominates the other communities which were forcibly incorporated long ago. The obvious examples of such 'dominant-ethnic' states are France, Britain, Spain, Russia and Sweden, all of which have one dominant 'core' ethnic community and one or more small, subordinate ones.[6] We find this pattern also in southeast Asia — an area colonised over long periods by France, Britain, Spain and Holland — in countries like Burma, Malaysia, Indonesia, Vietnam and the Philippines, which tend to have dominant core communities and several smaller peripheral ones.[7] And, in this respect, both areas contrast with some East European states — East Germany, Hungary, Poland, Greece — where the ethnic minorities are so tiny as to constitute no political or demographic problem for the state.

Now this same contrast between homogeneous and heterogeneous ethnic composition can be found within the fourth pattern of national formation, that of state-based territorialisms. At the more homogeneous end of the scale, such as we find in parts of Latin America, European rule has led to the formation of territorially-based states through a process of division along the lines of the Spanish administration. The national loyalties that have resulted are, in turn, founded upon the unifying action of the state in its wars with other Latin American states, or in its policies of economic protection against Western imperialism.[8] In sub-Saharan Africa, on the other hand, as in India and Pakistan, there is a highly heterogeneous ethnic composition within the new states that were created in the wake of European expansion, so that most of these states may be rightly designated as 'polyethnic', lacking as they usually did a single core ethnic community around which the state could be formed, as it was within Western Europe.

With the significant exception of Somalia, African states today fall into the category of polyethnic state-based territorialisms, since they contain a host of ethnic communities of varying size and antiquity, and possess no common cultural base for what is, consequently, an essentially territorial type of community. Applied to Africa, the Western model has produced something of an anomaly, a state which aims to turn itself into a nation, and a set of old ethnic communities and nations aspiring, it is hoped, to become one new nation. True, in a few cases like the Kikuyu in Kenya or the Hausa in Nigeria, one ethnic community has taken the lead; yet their dominance has been partial and is often challenged; in no sense can they be said to enjoy that unquestioned superiority that for so long characterised the position of the English in Britain or the French within France. Their position is more like that of the Serbs in Yugoslavia, another genuinely polyethnic territorial state, who must continually reassert their control over the state apparatus in the face of ethnic restiveness from powerful communities.[9]

It has been argued that pre–colonial Africa was characterised by a balance between unitary mono–ethnic states like Somalia today and polyethnic territorial empires like Ethiopia.[10] If so, that balance has been radically altered by Western intervention. For the Western powers, at their European congresses, paid little attention to questions of ethnic demography in fixing the boundaries of their African empires, to suit their economic needs and prestige sentiments. As a result, ethnic groups like the Ewe or BaKongo were divided between different territorial states, and each such territory came to include a mosaic of different ethnic communities and tribes. So that it was in a double sense that the boundaries of the new states were alien: alien in origin and alien in execution. But, it is these same alien boundaries that alone endow African states with concrete meaning, since they fix their location and format. And only insofar as they possess location and format, can they enjoy international recognition and standing. For this reason, such polyethnic state-based territorialisms have become the norm in Africa and south Asia; they alone confer legitimacy on states which possess no other basis, whether it be in popular assent or cultural community. African states today derive their legitimacy largely from the circumstances of their origins in deliberate acts of creation – by aliens for alien purposes – and in the resulting location they enjoy. Hence, the extreme fragility and overdevelopment of African and Asian states today.

For, standing in blatant opposition to the pretensions of the territorial state and its panoply of administrative organs, are

the serried ranks of ethnic communities and nations that
compose it. There is no 'nation' that is, in any way, co-
extensive with the state's boundaries, or congruent with the
state's culture. Such a congruent and co-extensive nation is a
mere project today, a 'nation of intent' to be forged out of the
territorial state.[11] As in Western Europe, African rulers and
intelligentsia aim to create such nations, and merge the political culture of the state with the several ethnic cultures of the
peoples that compose it. But, unlike their Western absolutist
counterparts, they are handicapped, not only by the time
factor, but by the later historical period in which they must
act, a democratic era in which the twin ideals of national
dignity and development must be reconciled and attained.

If state and society face each across a gulf unknown in the
West, if the principles of territorial statehood and ethnic
culture so rarely coincide in Africa and Asia, the chances of
forging genuine 'political communities' such as the West has
been fortunate to enjoy are greatly reduced. However much
African intelligentsia may be committed to the ideal of a
territorial nation, the dilemmas of creating a political community in such unpropitious circumstances are daunting. Here
I will consider only two of them, the one concerned with
political myths, the other with centralisation and democracy.

Every nation and every state requires some powerful myths
to engender the necessary loyalty and solidarity. In one way or
another, these are historic; they focus on events and persons
that have shaped the historical destiny of the population or
area, and use them to explain the present circumstances of the
community and its future course. These myths also encapsu-
late collective ideals; they symbolise the goals and admired
qualities of the group. But, in the case of recent states in Africa
and Asia, a choice presents itself: between the recent history of
the territorial state and its predominantly political myths, and
the ancient histories of the many ethnic communities and their
mainly cultural myths. Both have their defects: political myths
rarely strike so deep a chord in the populace as cultural traditions, and recent territorial history may well contain episodes
that have aggrieved particular ethnic communities in the new
state. Besides, how many people were really involved in the
heroic struggle against colonialism, how many endured suf-

ferings in the national movement against foreign rule, and how much has the glorious moment of freedom meant to the majority of the rural population? For that is the core of recent territorial history; a history of and for the state, and largely of and for the intelligentsia and their allies. Can the sense of political community and civic liberty so dear to the intelligentsia be transmitted to all sections of the population? May not the very territorialism and the essentially political content of its myths actually divorce the elites from the mass of the people? Besides, a purely political culture of the territorial state, which has been inherited from the colonialists, inevitably carries the stigma of its alien origins and foreign culture. In such circumstances, the temptation to return to older traditions must be great.

But these, too, carry grave dangers for a sense of territorial community. If the intelligentsia try to appeal to traditional cultures and their ancient historical myths, they risk splitting the new states; for the ancient myths and traditions are ethnic ones, that include some and exclude others, and may even rekindle old antagonisms. To raise the spectre of 'tribalism', of ethnic consciousness, in order to mobilise enthusiams and create a sense of state-wide solidarity, is a self-defeating exercise, and testifies to the lack of roots of the state's purely political culture. With some exceptions, later African history and culture has been that of its ethnic communities or nations such as the Yoruba, Ganda or Zulu. To cultivate a distinctive 'African personality' and African community, radicals like Nkrumah, Senghor and Kenyatta have been forced to make concessions to traditional African cultures, particularly where they were concerned to combat the vices of a purely western route to nationhood, its materialism and excessive individualism. To give an African meaning to their chosen path of change, African leaders have often had to look to their past, an ethnic past, for guidance and inspiration; and like such neo-traditionalist radicals as Tilak in India or al-Afghani among the Arabs, they have necessarily turned back to the formerly despised traditional ethnic cultures of the rural masses, with all the attendant risks to the territorial integrity and administrative stability of the state.[12]

The other dilemma concerns the political goals and methods

necessary for forging territorial nations, in the context of these polyethnic states. The dilemma is this: to preserve the fragile state and its artificially-created territorial domain, the leaders must centralise the means of administration and coercion, and place a heavy emphasis upon the inviolability of the territorial status quo and the need for political order. They must also extend the scope and powers of the centre throughout the territory, and hence the position of its bureaucratic personnel. Moreover, to counteract any tendencies to ethnic fragmentation and secession, the leadership must strengthen the powers of central institutions, so as to instil a sense of loyalty and solidarity across the whole territory to the political community embodied in the state. On the other side, to forge a nation as a civic community requires a much higher level of public enthusiasm and commitment than would be needed for purely ethnic and cultural allegiances. After all, the territorial nation is at present only a dream, which requires the substance of popular solidarity to turn it into a reality. It is also something remote and alien, which has to be fleshed out around the skeletal structures of an impersonal bureaucracy. To inspire people to make sacrifices for the ideals of development and national dignity, to get them to raise productivity, man institutions efficiently and improve a weak infrastructure, the masses need to be mobilised and educated and politicised. But mobilisation and politicisation may well rekindle the fires of ethnic conflict, because the prevailing communities within most African, and many Asian, states are ethnic in nature with strongly ethnocentric sentiments and outlooks. Therefore to tap the sources of popular zeal and commitment can jeopardise the stability and integrity of recently-formed states, which have no real basis in popular assent. The moment the intelligentsia seek a broader base within the populace, especially among the peasantry, they must face the prospect of cultural and ethnic, as well as class, divisions which may imperil, not only their own position, but that of the territorial state as a whole. Examples of just this dilemma can be found in Pakistan and Bangladesh, in Nigeria, in Angola and in Ethiopia today.

These are the kinds of problems that have made the intelligentsia 'play safe' by backing military-bureaucratic regimes of the kind that a succession of coups have installed in the last two decades in both Africa and Asia.[13] Military takeovers have a variety of grounds, which have included ethnic conflict in places like Uganda and Nigeria; while a good many more find one of their main justifications in the prevention of ethnic schism. Amin, Afrifa, Gowon and Mobutu have all benefited by ethnic strife; and all have thrown their weight behind the preservation of the territorial state, and the political status quo, at the cost of popular participation and social development. They have also testified to the popularity of an *étatiste* rather than collectivist type of nationalism, and to territorial nations based upon military-bureaucratic institutions forging a political community from the top downwards rather than risk ethnic rivalries by trying to mobilise the masses at the grassroots.

Military-bureaucratic nationalisms appear to have several advantages over the 'liberal' and mass-mobilising 'collectivist' types of nationalism. They are, to begin with, historically economical and convenient. In their hands, all the institutions built up by the colonial powers are retained or restored, and sometimes, as in Zaire, even the administrative divisions.[14] They represent a throwback to colonialism and its gubernatorial style, only this time the authoritarianism is military, so that military-bureaucratic regimes avoid innovations that can threaten the political order, and tend to work with the existing bureaucracy, and the more successful ones try to convert themselves into largely bureaucratic regimes, forsaking the military role, like Nasser and Mobutu.[15] Given the prior existence and authority of the bureaucracy, and the relative inexperience of many officers in administrative matters, it is easy to see why pragmatic considerations tend to outweigh ideological ones and so reinforce the institutions and ethos of the colonial state.

In the second place, there is a close affinity between a military-bureaucratic regime and ethos and the needs of a territorial state. Security and territorial integrity provide the *raison d'etre* of any army, and the state similarly requires a 'neutral custodian' in the form of depoliticised bulwark of authority. This also fits in well with the army's usual self-image as an impartial guardian and reservoir of latent patriotism, a professional shield for the nation while it grows into a unitary body of citizens, and in some cases a useful building-block for citizenship.[16] Hence the military format and attitude is closely attuned to the needs of a state-based territorial nationalism.

Thirdly, military-bureaucratic regimes provide important channels of mobility for the professional stratum. As the intelligentsia-in-arms, the military are themselves imbued with the values of professionalism, even if they are not always the modernising agent that they are sometimes portrayed to be.[17] Yet their professionalism allied them closely to the interests of the intelligentsia as a whole, and their acquisition of power tends to promote those interests, since their regimes require a continuous supply of trained personnel and new recruits from the schools, colleges and institutes, if the administrative machine is to function smoothly. Given their commitment to centralised planning and development 'from the top downwards', the military must fund education and the professions to ensure sufficient trained people to oversee the economy and social services, fields in which they themselves have few skills.

Finally, it is the military who are often most sensitive to external approval or pressure, since their main reference group is usually their ex-colonial mentor, in whose codes and colleges the officers have been trained. Their self-image as a fighting force, but even more the image of their society and government abroad, is of especial concern to them; and in this they converge with other sections of the intelligentsia who may also have travelled and studied abroad, and who have acquired a sense of comparative efficiency as products of westernised education, and whose reference groups are often their counterparts in other countries.[18] It is the military, especially, who reflect the wider concern for national dignity in the international status system.

Of course, military-bureaucratic regimes carry dangers and suffer from critical defects. One of these is an excessive concern with the interests of external bourgeoisies, even at the cost of much-needed internal reforms. Pragmatism here may generate some economic development, but this is often achieved at the cost of wider social development and redistribution. In fact, their ties with external groups, and concern for the state's image, often leads the military to accord greater scope for foreign economic interests. Military regimes also tend to neglect socioeconomic reform and the plight of the disprivileged because of their need to rely on bureaucratic expertise and their political conservatism. Huntington has characterised the military as conservative realists in their concern for national stability and their puritanical zeal for order and obedience; but that is not only a product of army training and ethos, but also of their commitment to centralised government and territorialism.[19] Centralism also makes it difficult for the military to deal with popular grievances, and that is one reason for the succession of coups witnessed in several African and Asian countries, as different strata and ethnic groups fail to receive what they consider to be their due.

All these limitations of military-bureaucratic regimes impede the formation of genuine territorial nations, the main legitimation of any centralising government. The frequency of military-bureaucratic regimes in Africa testifies to the near-impossibility of squaring the western territorial state with a democratic and popular mobilisation within fragile polyethnic milieux. Clearly the intelligentsia have preferred the evils of curtailing freedoms through excessive bureaucracy, to the dangers of class struggle and ethnic schism which hasty but divisive mobilisation so easily brings. It can be argued that the most successful military regimes are also the most civilianised and 'colonial' in their methods of curbing ethnic conflict. They differ from their colonial models only in their fervent commitment to an economic nationalism, which allows them greater room for manoeuvre at home and abroad. Acheampong in Ghana, and even more Mobutu in Zaire, have been careful to cultivate the educated elite while inculcating an ardent territorial nationalism; in the case of Zaire, this has included the use of the term 'citoyen' as the official mode of address.[20] Though the actual policies of military regimes have varied greatly — from Amin's erratic rejection of foreign economic interests and brutal Africanisation policies to the careful balancing of competitive group interests by Mobutu, Gowon or Acheampong — they have all sought to stabilise the territorial status quo while favouring their own special ethnic or social group interests. In this respect as in others, the military are just as much trapped within the dilemmas of trying to square territorial statehood with heterogeneous social and cultural nations as any other sector of the African and Asian intelligentsia.

Perhaps the sole advantage of an *étatiste* type of nationalism which military regimes so plainly exemplify is their firm commitment to centralised territorialism. Not many members of the intelligentsia, whatever their own ethnic commitments, are prepared to face up to a totally 'balkanised' Africa or Asia; of that, they feel, there is already sufficient. Their continual political preoccupation is exactly the dangers inherent in such 'tribalism' and the need to take stern measures, if necessary, to curb it; and in this they again look back to the European experience, notably that of Yugoslavia and its neighbours, which they contrast unfavourably with the 'orderly' and 'viable' political development of the West.[21] Once again, it is the West that provides, by its 'successful' historical example, a political heritage and model for future development. There is little doubt that most African and Asian leaders hope to emulate the West in this crucial respect, and ensure a high degree of congruence between state and nation, even if this means neglecting the goals of social development. As always, the political kingdom comes first.

But that in itself poses a fundamental problem. It is not simply developmental or social failures that impair the ability of latterday absolutist regimes to inspire and organise an effective political community or 'territorial nation'; the very concepts and derived practices are so alien and remote from the everyday lives and experiences of most of the population, that the 'western' territorial state must impose itself on African and Asian societies with even greater force and drive than its European predecessors, both within and outside Europe. Ethnic ties having only recently freed themselves in the towns from their kinship moorings, popular resistance to 'alien' rule by a small urban bureaucratic and westernised elite is bound to be much more tenacious and widespread. And given the 'spoils' system in most African and Asian states, by which the political kingdom is the almost exclusive means for attaining wealth and other values for specific factions and groups, and those who lack that power are thereby deprived of other benefits, there appear to be few grounds for optimism for the early formation of territorial nations in those continents.

Even the attempt to legitimate the western route and the territorial state by appealing to African or Asian precedents in distant empires — of Ashoka, of Ghana, Sudan and Mali — appears somewhat artificial and contrived, despite the very real psychological and cultural benefits such appeals may confer. The fact is that the colonial intrusion came as a sort of hiatus in the continuity of African and Asian historical experience, and it has imprinted itself so markedly on the social consciousness of most groups that the 'West' must continue to provide the language of discourse and perception in the political experience of Asians and Africans today and their main reference group for decades to come. Clearly, the dilemmas of political change which spring from this confrontation between alien ideals and structures and local cultures and communities which they seek to transform, will continue to beset African and Asian intelligentsias and their allies; for, not only the concept of the 'post-colonial state' itself, but the very ideals of development and national dignity are of alien derivation and inspiration, however much they have become assimilated locally. Their fervent pursuit by political leaders of every persuasion in the 'Third World' surely testifies to the attractions of Western ideals and frameworks in areas that have quite different social formations and cultural ideals.

In this process of transplantation, adaptation and fusion of different cultures and political forms, politicised intelligentsia play a decisive but ambiguous role. They have, of course, adopted many of the ideals and perceptions of their European mentors, if only through the language of their education; and they have more or less consciously selected elements from rival European traditions to fit the situations of their communities, as they perceived them. But, because they suffer social isolation and a crisis of cultural identity, they have often recoiled from full-scale acceptance of Western models, and sought instead to experiment with new ways of forging political community and novel forms of political ideology and social reform. They hope, by these means, to overcome the gulf created by their professional training and western education between their own outlook and that of their peasantries, who continue to form the bulk of the population. The danger, as we saw, is that such experiments with social mobilisation, unaccompanied by the more gradual processes of political socialisation, threaten both the stability of the territorial state itself, the bulwark of their own power, and also the unity and position of the intelligentsia, the only political stratum capable, at present, of exercising authority and ensuring political order compatible with the global system of states.

No doubt, the gradual formation and rise of new classes in several African and Asian states will challenge the present political ascendancy of the intelligentsia. Their representatives will either be incorporated within the present structures, or will ally themselves with one section of the intelligentsia against another, to achieve some measure of political power for their class. Either way, they will have to work with and through the territorial state and its professionalised bureaucracy; and either way, they too will have to face the more basic problems of ethnic discontinuity and popular mobilisation within the framework of post-colonial statehood. In other words, new lines of stratification only serve to complicate, but never remove, the deeper vertical differentiations which threaten the very existence of any political community which can mediate between African and Asian territorial states and ethnic nations.

How likely, then, are the state-based nationalisms of Africa and Asia to achieve their goal of territorial nations? They have one advantage over their European predecessors within Europe, in that the state itself is well formed and its territory clearly demarcated (with some historical exceptions), and the principle of territorial integrity is widely accepted and sanctioned by international bodies. Their grave disadvantage vis-a-vis their Western predecessors is the multiplicity and sheer diversity of their ethnic and national composition — the vastly differing size, scale, location and cultures of their ethnic communities and nations. Worse still, African and Asian leaders must work out their objectives in an age of nationalism and democratic mobilisation, in which the principle of popular sovereignty can be invoked for every small community that feels starved of due representation and ready for self-determination and autonomy. Unfortunately, though in the past such ethnic nationalisms aided the efforts of territorial nationalists, they show every sign of dividing the intelligentsia along ethnic and communal lines and thwarting the centralising efforts of political leaders to forge a truly territorial nation with a uniform political culture. Even the more realistic goal of a plural and possibly federal state calls for sophisticated and stable leadership over a long period, and one able to increase the stake of different ethnic groups and classes within the territorial political community. Undoubtedly, the attempt to ensure some degree of 'fit' between the western territorial state and local cultural communities in Africa and Asia, constitutes the most difficult and pressing task facing the intelligentsia in the future.

Notes

1 The Western Model

1 On such a transition, cf. Baran (1957) and Taylor (1979), and the discussion in the next chapter.
2 Mainly by the 'dependency' theorists, starting with Frank (1967); cf. also the essay by O'Brien in Oxaal (1975).
3 An approach that stems from Tonnies' and Durkheim's perspectives, and underlies many of the essays in that influential work on socioeconomic development, Hoselitz and Moore's *Industrialisation and Society*, Mouton, The Hague 1963.
4 For example, Parsons (1961) and (1966); Smelser (1968); Levy (1966); and Bellah (1964). For a critical discussion, see A. D. Smith (1973).
5 Shils (1964).
6 Shils (1960).
7 Eisenstadt (1965).
8 Eisenstadt (1970) and (1973), esp. Part II.
9 For a fuller discussion, see A. D. Smith (1976), ch.4.
10 Almond (1966); Apter (1963) and (1965); and Binder (1964).
11 D. Apter: 'Political religion in the new nations', in Geertz (1963); and for a critique, see A. D. Smith (1973b).
12 Lerner (1958).
13 Ibid., 46.
14 Ibid., 50.
15 Ibid., 55.
16 Ibid., 47; cf. also Polk (1965) for a Middle Eastern application.
17 Ibid., 46.
18 Ibid., 47.
19 On the idea of 'cultural significance', see Weber (1949), Part II.
20 For fuller discussions, see A. D. Smith (1971), ch.5; and Peacock (1966).
21 Deutsch (1966), 97.
22 Ibid., 101.
23 Ibid., 130-34, 142-48.
24 cf. also Deutsch and Foltz (1963) and Deutsch (1961), for these ideas.
25 But, cf. Koht (1947) and others in Tipton (1972), who date the origins of these processes much earlier; for a comprehensive historical analysis, cf. Seton-Watson (1977), esp. chh. 2-4.
26 Connor (1972); also Ashworth (1977) and (1978) for some of these ethnic minorities.
27 W. Petersen: 'On the Subnations of Western Europe', in Glazer & Moynihan (1975).
28 See the essays in Esman (1977), esp. by Connor and Esman.
29 Even in ancient Greece, where polis loyalty clashed with Hellenic; on this, see Andrewes (1965), and for the Italian case, Waley (1969).
30 See Steinberg (1976).
31 This has been the reluctant conclusion of many an anti-Western nationalist regime in Asia or Africa, confronted by a multiplicity of languages in their

domain. On the role of language, cf. Haugen (1966) and the essays in Fishman (1968).
32 Tilly (1975).
33 Ibid., 27.
34 For these 'ethnic' definitions of the 'nation', cf. Snyder (1954); Akzin (1964); and A. D. Smith (1973a), section 1.
35 On this, see Mayo (1974) and Esman (1977).
36 Tilly, *op. cit.*, 17–31.
37 Ibid., 42.
38 Ibid., 44–6; and Wallerstein (1974).
39 Poggi (1978), ch.1.

2   Imperialism and Colonialism

1 Geiger (1967) examines some of the main differences in Africa and Asia.
2 Wolf (1973).
3 Tilly (1975), 636–8.
4 Hobson (1902).
5 Lenin (1916); and cf. Brewer (1980), ch.5.
6 See Avineri (1968), 162–74, on the universality of capitalism in Marx's theory.
7 Hilferding (1910); cf. the penetrating critique in Brewer, *op. cit.*, ch.4.
8 Ibid., cited in Fieldhouse (1967), 82.
9 Ibid., cited in Fieldhouse (1967), 84.
10 See, *inter alia,* Fieldhouse (1966) and Lichtheim (1971).
11 Staley (1935), cited in Fieldhouse (1967), 15; A.J.P. Taylor (1956), cited in Fieldhouse (1967), 128.
12 Nurkse (1961), cited in Fieldhouse (1967), 160–2.
13 Wallerstein (1974). For other accounts, cf. Frank (1967) and Magdoff (1969).
14 On the interaction of European motives and African situations, see Robinson & Gallagher (1961), esp. 462–7.
15 Fieldhouse (1967), xiv–xvi, 192–4.
16 Kedourie (1971), 4.
17 Worsley (1964), 49.
18 Ibid., 45.
19 Mannoni (1956); Fanon (1961).
20 For such 'dependency' theories, cf. O'Brien (1975); Roxborough (1976).
21 Montagne (1952).
22 See Crowder (1968) for a detailed study of West African systems.
23 Balandier (1966).
24 Forster (1924), ch.5.
25 See July (1967); Wilson (1968).
26 Hodgkin (1956), 52.
27 See Young (1965) on the *evolués* and social changes.
28 See W. H. Lewis (1965), for the effects of such cultural assimilation.
29 Hodgkin, *op.cit.*, 33–40; and Crowder, *op.cit.*
30 Hodgkin, *op.cit.*, 40–43, 45–7; for Nigeria, see Coleman (1958).
31 Nottingham & Rosberg (1966); Rotberg (1962).
32 Ranger (1979) contains articles surveying settler influences.
33 For a more sophisticated ranking, cf. Eisenstadt (1968).
34 For a critique, see Fieldhouse, *op.cit.*, xiv–xix, 187–94.

3 Nationalism in Africa

1 Hodgkin (1956), 23.
2 Kautsky (1962), 39.
3 Gellner (1964), ch.7.
4 Nairn (1977), 101-2; for the Leninist tradition as a whole, cf. Davis (1967) and (1978).
5 See Acton (1862). The most effective statements of this critique are Kedourie (1960) and Minogue (1967).
6 Coleman (1958), ch.7.
7 Apter (1963b).
8 de Klerk (1975); and Skinner (1964).
9 Elsewhere I have discussed the definition of nations and nationalism, and proposed that we define nationalism as an ideological movement for the attainment and maintenance of autonomy, cohesion and identity of a social group, some of whose members conceive it to be an actual or potential nation; on this, see A. D. Smith (1973a) and (1979), ch.4.
10 On these, see Lanternari (1965) and Burridge (1969).
11 Cohn (1957) vividly describes several medieval movements.
12 Sundkler (1948).
13 Balandier (1955).
14 H. S. Wilson (1968), Introduction, 40-41.
15 Balandier (1953); for some Asian parallels, cf. Burridge (1969) and Kolarz (1954).
16 Shepperson and Price (1958).
17 Worsley (1968), 2nd edition.
18 For a fuller discussion, see A. D. Smith (1979), ch.2.
19 Shepperson (1960).
20 Hodgkin (1956), 100.
21 Geiss (1974), ch.8; and Shepperson (1953).
22 On this expansion, see Hodgkin (1956), 63-70; also Gutkind (1962).
23 Elkan (1960) discusses the various factors.
24 For the Ivory Coast, see Zolberg (1964); for Nigeria, Coleman (1958); and more generally, Lloyd (1967), 68-81.
25 Geiss (1974), 288-9, 368-9.
26 On the Belgian Congo, see Young (1965); and on French policies, Crowder (1968).
27 For these figures, see Coleman (1954).
28 Kimble (1963); and more generally, Lloyd (1967), ch.5.
29 On these early figures, see July (1967); also Nicol (1969).
30 Geiss (1974), 288; Hodgkin (1956), 139-42.
31 On French policies and territories, see W. H. Lewis (1965).
32 For these figures, see Lloyd, *op.cit.*, 148-9.
33 For an Indian parallel, cf. McCulley (1966); and generally, Kedourie (1971), 81-90.
34 For this transformation, and the popular participation it involved, see Marwick (1974).
35 On these, see Little (1965).
36 On the territorial nature of the state in Africa, see Montagne (1952) and Emerson (1960); and for Europe, the articles in Tilly (1975), especially Finer's.
37 On African Party rule, cf. Kilson (1963). Israel affords a good parallel of the movement organising a 'counter-state', cf. Halpern (1961) and Elon (1971).
38 On these influences, see Hodgkin (1961). The Ewe and Somali are the main

exceptions; on the Ewe, see Welch (1966).
39   Hodgkin (1964); and generally, July (1967).
40   Rotberg (1967); also Kilson (1958).
41   On Switzerland, cf. Steinberg (1976); it appears to date the most successful case, perhaps the only one, of achieving the 'nation' through a sense of political community which 'transcends' the ethnic (Alemannic) heritage.
42   On the CPP, see Austin (1964); and generally, on western influences, Hodgkin (1956), 155 sqq.
43   Nairn (1977), 340.
44   On 'nation-building', cf. Deutsch & Foltz (1963).
45   Mazrui (1966), ch.3.
46   Legum (1962).
47   Ajayi (1960); Esedebe (1970).
48   Legum (1962), Introduction; the quotation is from Claude McKay's poem, *Outcast*.
49   On this Zionism, cf. Hertzberg (1960); and A. D. Smith (1979), ch.5.
50   For the Christian missions, cf. Ajayi (1964).
51   For the distinction in Latin America, cf. Laclau (1971).
52   On this business history, cf. A. G. Hopkins (1976).
53   On the Kikuyu and Ewe, cf. Rosberg and Nottingham (1966) and Welch (1966); and on Mali, Apter (1963a).

4   Ethnicity and Class

1   This was a common theme of African leaders like Sekou Toure, Senghor and Nkrumah in the 1960s, for which see Worsley (1964) and for an Indian parallel, cf. Dumont's (1970) brilliant contrast between Western individualism and Indian communitarianism.
2   For the Slavophile conceptions, cf. Thaden (1964); for the communitarian ideal of Tonnies and Durkheim, cf. Nisbet (1965) and, for Rousseau, Durkheim (1965) and Baron (1960), ch.2.
3   Especially with the Black revolt of the 1960s, cf. Silberman (1964) and Draper (1970).
4   For these views, see also Lloyd (1967), ch.11.
5   Neuberger (1977).
6   On such 'neo-colonialism', see Amin (1973).
7   For an excellent case study, see Rothchild (1972).
9   Evans-Pritchard (1940); Wagner (1940).
9   Vansina (1966), 14.
10   Murdock (1959).
11   Richards (1940); Mair (1962).
12   Middleton (1958).
13   Gluckman (1961) and (1968); cf. also Mercier (1965).
15   King (1976).
16   This definition is adapted from the Appendix of Coleman (1958); but it also takes into account the 'political' usages of most of the contributors to the Fortes and Evans-Pritchard (1940) volume. For the Israelite confederation, cf. Noth (1960).
17   This definition, again, resembles that given by Coleman (1958) to the term 'nationality'.

18   Weber (1947), 176.
19   For fuller discussions of the concept of 'nation', cf. Zernatto (1944), Deutsch (1966), ch.1, and Rustow (1967), ch.1.
20   For this definition, see A. D. Smith (1973a) and (1979), ch.4.
21   Cohen (1969), 190.
22   On Ethiopia, cf. Hess (1966); Markovitz (1977).
23   Lewis (1963).
24   Rothchild (1972); Mazrui (1975); Ashworth (1980), 132-9.
25   Turner (1972).
26   Ashworth (1978), 34-38; Davidson et al. (1976).
27   Lyon (1980).
28   Panter-Brick (1970).
29   On the range of ethnic minorities, cf. Andersen et al. (1967) and Ashworth (1977, 1978, 1980). Bangladesh has been the only really successful postWar example of ethnic separatism from a newly 'created' state. Others like the Ibo, Kurds, Eritreans, Moro, Shan, Ewe and BaKongo have tried, unsuccessfully so far.
30   Including most contributors to Olorunsola (1972).
31   As has Petersen (1975); for a critique of this tendency, cf. Connor (1977) and (1978).
32   Geertz (1963); Silvert (1963).
33   On these factors, see Gellner (1973), and Argyle (1976).
34   On the political irrelevance of 'size', see Hobsbawm (1977); and for the variety of African 'peoples', see Ottenberg (1960).
35   Argyle (1969).
36   Young (1965); and Turner (1972).
37   Neuberger (1976).
38   For which, cf. Lloyd (1967); and for Central Asian examples, cf. Bennigsen and Quelquejay (1966).
39   Rothchild (1972).
40   Coleman (1958).
41   Sklar (1966); Wallerstein (1960); and Little (1965).
42   For European examples, cf. Esman (1977).
43   On the counterpoint of class and ethnicity, see Lijphart (1977); for great power attitudes, see Said & Simmons (1976) and A. D. Smith (1979).
44   For the differences between Eastern and Western Europe, see Seton-Watson (1977).
45   Marx (1976), 91.
46   Hindess and Hirst (1975); Hobsbawm (1964), Introduction.
47   Amin (1981); and on 'feudalism' in Latin America, cf. Laclau (1971).
48   On this, see Hobsbawm (1964), Introduction.
49   Nadel (1942); M. G. Smith (1960).
50   Maquet (1961); and Mason (1971).
51   Mair (1962); also Apter (1963b).
52   Goody (1971).
53   On feudalism generally, cf Coulborn (1956); Bloch (1961); and Hall (1962).
54   Coleman (1954); Kimble (1963).
55   Kilson (1970); Fallers (1965); Markovitz (1977), 153-72.
56   Markovitz, *op.cit.*, ch.4.
57   On African workers, cf. Markovitz, *op.cit.*, ch.8; Arrighi and Saul (1973), ch.3; Peace (1975); and Gutkind, Cohen and Copans (1977).
58   See Lloyd (1967); Markovitz, *op.cit.*
59   See Davies (1966); Sandbrook and Cohen (1975).
60   Davies, *op.cit.*, and Markovitz, *op.cit.*, ch.8.

61 Epstein (1958).
62 Lerner (1958); Saul (1973).
63 But cf. Markovitz, *op.cit.*, ch.7; Arrighi & Saul (1973).
64 Hunter (1962); Kitching (1980).
65 Gans (1977); Esman (1977).

5 State and Intelligentsia

1 Mannheim (1940).
2 J. H. Kautsky (1962), Introduction.
3 J. H. Kautsky (1968).
4 Gellner (1964), ch.7.; also idem (1973).
5 For a critique, cf. A.D. Smith (1971), ch.6; and idem (1981), ch.3.
6 Shils (1960).
7 Gouldner (1979).
8 cf. Gella (1976) for studies of these two groups.
9 Hunter (1962).
10 H. & M. Smythe (1960).
11 Lloyd (1966).
12 Van den Berghe (1973), esp. 75, 153-5.
13 Markovitz (1977), 224.
14 *Ibid.*, ch.6. esp. 204-15.
15 *Ibid.*, 209.
16 For the marxist concept of class, see Ossowski (1962) and Giddens (1973).
17 First (1970), esp. 95-7; Markovitz (1977), ch.6.
18 Lloyd (1967), ch.5.
19 Lloyd (1966), esp. 56-7; Hodgkin (1964).
20 Kimble (1963), esp. 62.
21 Markovitz (1977), ch.3, analyses the impact of the metropolitan bourgeoisie; for East Africa, cf. Brett (1973) and Kitching (1980).
22 Jacoby (1973); Gouldner (1979).
23 See Crowder (1968) and Geiss (1974).
24 On this process, see, inter alia, Wallerstein (1961) and Cowan (1964).
25 Alavi (1972).
26 *Ibid.*, 61.
27 *Ibid.*, 62.
28 For some exceptions, such as northern Nigeria, see above, chapter 4.
29 Saul (1979), ch.8.
30 *Ibid.*, ch.8; cf. also Goulbourne (1980).
31 For such intraelite conflicts, see Wallerstein (1965).
32 For the geopolitical constraints, see Nettl & Robertson (1968), Pt.11.
33 Kiernan (1976); and Hodgkin (1956), Pt.1.
34 For some of these Islamic strongholds, see W. H. Lewis (1965).
35 In this respect, the French were partial exceptions; see above chapter 2.
36 Enloe (1980), ch.2.
37 Lyon (1980).
38 For analyses of these effects, see Mannoni (1956) and Fanon (1961).
39 See Geiss (1974), ch.15; Legum (1962).
40 Ajayi (1960); Geiss, *op.cit.*

41 On this collectivism, see Lloyd (1967), ch.11; Friedland & Rosberg (1964).
42 On this, cf. Enloe (1980) and Turner (1972), especially the 'invented' case of the Bangala in the Belgian Congo.
43 Sklar (1963); Panter-Brick (1970), esp. Luckham.
44 Neuberger (1976).
45 For this distinction, see A. D. Smith (1981), ch.6.
46 For such ideologues, see Feuer (1975).
47 Originally a Herderian conception, see Berlin (1976); on its application in Africa, see July (1967) and Mazrui (1966), ch.3.
48 Weber (1947), 176.
49 For the educational and purifying activities of intellectuals, see Shils (1960) and Mosse (1976).
50 On the French example during the revolution of 1789-94, see Herbert (1972) and A.D. Smith (1976); for its African legacy, see Hodgkin (1961).
51 On such 'bearer' strata, see Weber (1965), chh. 6-8.
52 For this 'multi-class' appeal, see Nairn (1977), ch.2; and A. D. Smith (1976), Introduction and essay by Kiernan.

6 Populism and Communism

1 See Kohn (1955) for the distinction between 'Western' rationalist and 'Eastern' organic and collectivist modes of nationalism.
2 For the 'mass mobilising' kind of nationalism in Africa, see Apter (1963a); and for 'reformist' and revolutionary' nationalisms, cf. Davidson (1975), chh.2,5.
3 For their theories, see Kemilainen (1964) and Baron (1960), ch.2.
4 For this official Marxist position, see Shaheen (1956).
5 See, inter alia, Davis (1967), ch.3; and Avineri (1969).
6 Marx and Engels (1959), 26.
7 Ibid., 12.
8 Heller (n.d.), esp. 15-17; and Cummins (1980), 17-18.
9 Cummins, *op.cit.*, 19, for the first quotation; and Davis, *op.cit.* 17, for the second.
10 On Engels' specific contribution, especially as editor responsible for international affairs on the *Neue Rheinische Zeitung* in 1848-49, cf. ch.2 of the interesting account by Cummins (1980).
11 F. Engels: 'Democratic Panslavism, I', *Neue Rheinische Zeitung*, 15 February 1849, cited in Cummins, *op.cit.*, 37.
12 On this whole question, see Rosdolsky (1964).
13 F. Engels: 'The Magyar Struggle', *Neue Rheinische Zeitung* No. 194, 13 January 1849, cited in Cummins, *op.cit.*, 38.
14 K. Marx: *The Civil War in France* (1871), cited in Cummins, *op.cit.*, 33.
15 On the details of their views, see Davis (1967), chh. 2-3; and Cummins, *op.cit.*, chh.2, 4, 6.
16 On their influence, see Avineri (1969); also Cummins, *op.cit.*, ch.3.
17 A brief discussion of Rosa Luxemburg's views is contained in Davis, *op.cit.*, 134-39.
18 Lenin (1967), 2-4; cf. Davis (1978), ch.3.
19 Fieldhouse (1967) and Lenin (1916) and (1920).
20 Lenin (1967), 6, where the merging of nations within a truly socialist federation is proclaimed to be the ultimate goal.

21 For Bauer and Renner, see Davis, *op.cit.*, 149–65; for Stalin's critique, see Stalin (1936); and Bauer (1924) on the nation as a "community of fate".
22 See A. D. Smith (1979), ch.5.
23 Averini (1968), esp. chh.5,7.
24 For the German Romantic doctrines of education and struggle, see Kohn (1965).
25 Marx (1967), 301–14.
26 Johnson (1969).
27 Especially in Cuba; see Leiden & Schmitt (1968), ch.10.
28 As in China and Vietnam, on which see Scalapino (1969).
29 On this educated class, see Hess (1966); and for the revolution, see Halliday and Molyneux (1981).
30 Ashworth (1978), 34–38; for a detailed history of Angola, see Davidson (1975a), esp. 51–55, 66–79.
31 Worsley (1970); Arrighi and Saul (1973), ch.4; Rosberg and Callaghey (1979).
32 On this, see J. H. Kautsky (1968); and Gellner & Ionescu (1970).
33 On modern 'peasant wars', see Wolf (1973).
34 Gellner & Ionescu, *op.cit.*, esp. Worsley, Saul and Stewart.
35 cf. Warren (1980) for a critique of populist nationalism; an example from Europe of this progression is the Rumanian early fascism of Codreanu, on which see E. Weber (1966).
36 On this see Marx (1967) and Avineri (1968).
37 Wolf, *op.cit.*, and Barrington Moore (1967) analyse these movements.
38 Draper (1965); and Leiden and Schmitt, *op.cit.*, ch.10.
39 For a radical critique of such policies, cf. Saul (1979).
40 Debray (1968).
41 Huntington (1968), ch.5.
42 On Somalia and Ethiopia, see Lewis (1980), chh.9–10; for the Russian nationalities' policies, cf. Pipes (1975).
43 See Lowenthal (1962); and for African examples, Rosberg and Callaghey (1979).
44 For this distinction, cf. Yapp (1979).
45 Johnson (1962).
46 Burks (1961); and Lederer (1969).
47 Davidson (1975a); and Davidson, Slovo and Wilkinson (1976).
48 On this see Hodgkin (1961).
49 Lewis, *op.cit.*, 233 sqq.
50 Ibid., 209–211.
51 As Connor (1972) and (1978) has shown.
52 On communist limitations in Africa, cf Seton-watson (1978).
53 On this tradition see Cohler (1970).
54 For Cabral's own analysis, see Cabral (1974), 46 sqq.; and in general, Lyon (1980), to which this section is indebted.
55 Lyon, *op.cit.*, 158; and cf. Davis (1978), ch.8.

7 Forging Territorial Nations

1 Seton-Watson (1977), ch.2.
2 On this, see Tilly (1975).
3 Seton-Watson, *op.cit.*, ch.5.; and Kohn (1957a).
4 Sugar and Lederer (1969); and Sugar (1980).

5   For these developments in the later Middle Ages, see the essays in Tipton (1972); also Strayer (1963).

6   For concise summaries of these cases, see Seton-Watson, *op.cit.*, esp. ch.2.

7   On the area, generally, see Osborne (1971); and, more specifically, Wertheim (1956) and Roff (1967).

8   See Masur (1966).

9   On the background, see Burks (1961), ch. 6.

10 Lewis (1980), ch.10.

11 Rotberg (1967) uses this expression for sub-Saharan African nationalisms.

12 Of course, African history has also revolved around conquest states and empires; but many of these, especially in West Africa, disappeared some centuries before the colonial intrusion; while colonialism itself often used ethnic cultural differences and latent antagonisms for its own ends. For the uses of the African heritage, see Ajayi (1960); and on Tilak and al-Afghani, see Adenwalla (1961) and Kedourie (1966).

13 Classic studies of military intervention and performance are those of Finer (1962) and Janowitz (1964).

14 Gutteridge (1975), 148.

15 On Nasser's regime, see Vatikiotis (1961).

16 On the role of armies in the growth of European states, see Finer (1975); and the studies in Bramson and Goethals (1964).

17 For a discussion of this question, see K. Hopkins (1966).

18 On this, see Gutteridge, *op.cit.*, ch.2; and Nettl and Robertson (1968), Part II.

19 Huntington (1957), esp. 29.

20 Gutteridge, *op.cit.*, 151.

21 Neuberger (1976).

Bibliography

Acton, Lord (1862): 'Nationality', in *The history of freedom and other essays*, edited by J.N. Figgis and R.V. Laurence, Macmillan, London 1919.

Adenwalla, M. (1961): 'Hindu concepts and the Gita in early Indian thought', in R.K. Sakai (ed): *Studies on Asia*, University of Nebraska Press, Lincoln 1961.

Ajayi, J.F.A. (1960): 'The place of African history and culture in the process of nation-building in Africa south of the Sahara', *Journal of Negro Education* 30, 1960, 206-13.

Ajayi, J.F.A. (1964): *Christian Missions in Nigeria, 1841-91; The making of a new elite*, Longman, London 1964.

Akzin, B. (1964): *State and Nation*, Hutchinson, London 1964.

Alavi, H. (1972): 'The state in post-colonial societies — Pakistan and Bangladesh', *New Left Review* 74, 1972, 59-81.

Almond, G. (1966): *Comparative Politics: a developmental approach*, Little, Brown, Boston 1966.

Amin, S. (1973): *Neo-colonialism in West Africa*, Penguin, Harmondsworth 1973.

Amin, S. (1981): *Class and Nation*, Heinemann, London 1981.

Andersen, C.W. von der Mehden, F.R. and Young, C. (1967): *Issues of Political Development*, Prentice-Hall, Englewood Cliffs 1967.

Andrewes, A. (1965): 'The growth of the city-state', in H. Lloyd-Jones (ed): *The Greek World*, Penguin, Harmondsworth 1965.

Apter, D. (1963): *Ghana in Transition*, Athenaeum, New York 1963.

Apter, D. (1963a): 'Political religion in the new nations', in C. Geertz (1963).

Apter, D. (1963b): 'The role of traditionalism in the political modernisation of Ghana and Uganda', *World Politics* 13, 1961, 45-68.

Apter, D. (1965): *The Politics of Modernisation*, Chicago University Press, Chicago 1965.

Argyle, W.J. (1969): 'European nationalism and African tribalism', in P. Gulliver (ed): *Tradition and transition in East Africa*, Pall Mall Press, London 1969.

Argyle, W.J. (1976): 'Size and Scale as factors in the development of nationalist movements', in A.D. Smith (1976).

Arrighi, G. & Saul, J. (1973): *Essays on the Political Economy of Africa*, Monthly Review Press, New York (1973).

Ashworth, (1977, 1978, 1980) (ed): *World Minorities*, Vol. I (1977); Vol II (1978); Vol. III (1980): *World Minorities in the Eighties*, Quartermaine House Ltd., Sunbury, Middlesex.

Austin, D. (1964): *Politics in Ghana, 1946–60*, Oxford University Press, London 1964.

Avineri, S. (1968): *The social and political thought of Karl Marx*, Cambridge University Press, Cambridge 1968.

Avineri, S. (1969): *Karl Marx on colonialism and modernisation*, Anchor Books, New York 1969.

Balandier, G. (1953): 'Nationalismes et messianismes en Afrique noire', *Cahiers Internationaux de Sociologie*, 14, 1953, 41–65.

Balandier, G. (1955): *Sociologie actuelle de l'Afrique noire*, Presses Universitaires de France, Paris 1955.

Balandier, G. (1966): 'The colonial situation', in Wallerstein, (1966).

Baran, P. (1957): *The Political Economy of Growth*, Penguin, Harmondsworth, 1957.

Baron, S. (1960): *Modern nationalism and religion*, Meridian Books, New York 1960.

Barrington-Moore, Jr. (1967): *Social origins of dictatorship and democracy*, Allen Lane, The Penguin Press, London 1967.

Bauer, O. (1924): *Die Nationalitätenfrage und die Sozialdemokratie*, 2nd ed'n. Brand, Vienna 1924.

Bellah, R. (1964): 'Religious evolution', *American Sociological Review* 29, 1964, 358–74.

Bennigsen, A. and Lemercier-Quelquejay, C. (1966): *Islam in the Soviet Union*, Pall Mall, London 1966.

Berlin, I. (1966): *Vico and Herder*, The Hogarth Press, London 1966.

Binder, L. (1964): *The Ideological Revolution in the Middle East.*, Wiley, New York, 1964.

Bloch, M. (1961): *Feudal Society*, Routledge and Kegan Paul Ltd., London 1961.

Bramson, L. & Goethals, G.L. (eds.) (1964): *War, studies from psychology, sociology, anthropology*, Basic Books, New York & London 1964.

Brett, E.A. (1973):   *Colonialism and underdevelopment in East Africa*, Heinemann, London.

Brewer, A. (1980):   *Marxist Theories of Imperialism*, Routledge and Kegan Paul, London.

Burks, R.V. (1961):   *The dynamics of communism in Eastern Europe* Princeton University Press, Princeton 1961.

Burridge, K. (1969):   *New Heaven, New Earth*, Basil Blackwell, Oxford 1969.

Cabral, A. (1974):   *Revolution in Guinea*, Stage 1, London 1974.

Cohen, A. (1969):   *Custom and Politics in urban Africa*, University of California Press, Berkeley & Los Angeles 1969.

Cohler, A. (1970):   *Rousseau and nationalism*, Basic Books, Inc. New York and London 1957.

Cohn, N. (1957):   *The Pursuit of the Millennium*, Secker and Warburg, London 1957.

Coleman, J.S. (1954):   'Nationalism in Tropical Africa', *American Political Science Review* 18, 1954, 404-26.

Coleman, J.S. (1958):   *Nigeria: Background to nationalism*, University of California Press, Berkeley & Los Angeles, 1958.

Connor, W. (1972):   'Nation-building or nation-destroying?', *World Politics* 24, 1972, 319-55.

Connor, W. (1977):   'Ethnonationalism in the First World', in Esman (1977).

Connor, W. (1978):   'A nation is a nation, is a state, in an ethnic group, is a . . . ' *Ethnic & Racial Studies* 1/4, 1978, 377-400.

Coulborn, R. (1956):   *Feudalism in history*, Princeton University Press, Princeton 1956.

Cowan, L.G. (1964):   *The dilemmas of African independence*, Walker & Company, New York 1964.

Crowder, M. (1968):   *West Africa under colonial rule*, Hutchinson & Co. London 1968.

Cummins, I. (1980):   *Marx, Engels and National Movements*, Croom Helm Ltd., London 1980.

Davidson, B. (1975):   *Can Africa Survive?* Heinemann, London 1975.

Davidson, B. (1975a):   *In the Eye of the Storm: Angola's People*, Penguin, Harmondsworth 1975.

Davidson, B., Slovo, J. and *Southern Africa, the new politics of revolution*, Wilkinson, A.R. (1976):   Penguin, Harmondsworth 1976.

Davies, I. (1966):   *African Trade Unions*, Penguin, Harmondsworth 1966.

Davis, H.B. (1967):   *Nationalism and Socialism*, Monthly Review Press, New York 1967.

Davis, H.B. (1978):   *Towards a Marxist Theory of Nationalism*, Monthly Review Press, New York 1978.

Debray, R. (1968):   *Revolution in the Revolution*, Penguin, Harmondsworth 1968.

Deutsch, K. (1961):   'Social mobilisation and political development', *American Political Science Review* 55, 1961, 493–514.

Deutsch, K. (1966):   *Nationalism and social communication*, 2nd rev. ed'n, M.I.T. Press, Cambridge, Mass. 1966.

Deutsch, K. & Foltz, W. (eds.) (1963):   *Nation–Building*, Atherton, New York 1963.

Draper, T. (1970):   *The re-discovery of Black nationalism*, Secker & Warburg, London 1970.

Dumont, L. (1970):   *Homo hierarchicus*, Weidenfeld & Nicolson, London 1970.

Durkheim, E. (1965):   *Montesquieu and Rousseau*, University of Michigan Press, Ann Arbor 1965.

Eisenstadt, S. (1965):   *Modernisation: Protest and Change*, Prentice-Hall, Englewood Cliffs 1965.

Eisenstadt, S. (1968):   'Some new looks at the problem of relations between traditional societies and modernisation', *Economic Development and Cultural Change* 16, 1968, 436–50.

Eisenstadt, S. (ed) (1970):   *Readings in social evolution and development*, Pergamon Press, Oxford & London 1970.

Eisenstadt, S. (1973):   *Tradition, Change and modernity*, Wiley, New York 1973.

Elkan, W. (1960):   *Migrants and proletarians*, Oxford University Press, London 1960.

Elon, A. (1972):   *The Israelis, Founders and Sons*, Weidenfeld & Nicolson, London 1971.

Emerson, R. (1960):   'Nationalism and political development', *Journal of Politics* 22, 1960, 3–28.

Emerson, R. (1963):   'Nation–building in Africa', in Deutsch & Foltz (1963).

Enloe, C. (1980):   *Ethnic Soldiers*, Penguin, Harmondsworth 1980.

Epstein, A.L. (1958):   *Politics in an urban African community*, Manchester University Press, Manchester 1958.

Esedebe, O. (1970):   'The origins and meanings of panAfricanism', *Presence Africaine* 73, 1970, 109–27.

Esman, M.J. (ed) (1977):   *Ethnic conflict in the Western world*, Cornell University Press, Ithaca and London 1977.

Evans-Pritchard, E. (1940):   *The Nuer*, Clarendon Press, Oxford 1940.

Fallers, L. (1965):   *Bantu Bureaucracy*, University of Chicago Press, Chicago 1965.

Fanon, F. (1961):   *Le damnés de la terre*, Maspero, Paris 1961.

Feuer, L.S. (1975):   *Ideology and the ideologists*, Basil Blackwell, Oxford 1975.

Fieldhouse, D. (1967):   *The theory of capitalist imperialism*, Longman, London 1967.

Finer, S. (1975):   'State- and nation-building in Europe: the role of the military', in Tilly (1975).

First, R. (1970):   *Power in Africa*, Pantheon, New York 1970.

Fishman, J. et al. (eds) (1968):   *Language problems of developing countries*, John Wiley, New York 1968.

Fortes, M. and Evans-Pritchard, E. (eds)(1940):   *African Political Systems*, Oxford University Press, London 1940.

Forster, E.M. (1924):   *A Passage to India*, Penguin, Harmondsworth 1924.

Frank, A.G. (1967):   *Capitalism and underdevelopment in Latin America*, Monthly Review Press, New York 1967.

Friedland, W.H. and Rosberg, C. G. (eds) (1964):   *African Socialism*, Oxford University Press, London 1964.

Gans, H. (1979):   'Symbolic ethnicity', *Ethnic and Racial Studies* 2, 1979, 1-20.

Geertz, C. (1963):   'The integrative revolution', in Geertz (ed) (1963).

Geertz, C. (ed) (1963):   *Old societies and new states; the quest for modernity in Africa and Asia*, Free Press, New York 1963.

Geiger, T. (1967):   *The conflicted relationship*, McGraw-Hill Book Company, New York 1967.

Geiss, I. (1974):   *The Pan-African Movement*, Methuen & Co., London 1974.

Gella, A. (ed) (1976):   *The intelligentsia and the intellectuals*, Sage Publications, Beverley Hills 1976.

Gellner, E. (1964):   *Thought and Change*, Weidenfeld & Nicolson, London 1964.

Gellner, E. (1973):   'Scale and nation', *Philosophy of the social sciences* 3, 1973, 1-17.

Gellner, E. & Ionescu, G. (eds) (1970):   *Populism, its meaning and national characteristics*, Weidenfeld & Nicolson, London 1970.

Giddens, A. (1973):   *The Class Structure of the Advanced Societies*, Hutchinson University Library, London 1973.

Glazer, D. and Moynihan, D. (eds) (1975):   *Ethnicity, theory and experience*, Harvard University Press, Cambridge, Mass. 1975.

Gluckman, M. (1940):   'The kingdom of the Zulu of South Africa', in Fortes and Evans-Pritchard (1940).

Gluckman M. (1961):   'Anthropological problems arising from the African Industrial Revolution', in A. Southall (ed): *Social Change in Modern Africa*, Oxford University Press, London 1961.

Gluckman, M. (1968):   'Tribalism in Modern British Central Africa', *Cahiers d'études Africaines* 1, 1968, 55-70.

Goody, J. (1971):   *Technology, Tradition and the State in Africa*, Oxford University Press, London 1971.

Goulbourne, H. (ed) (1980):   *Politics and the State in the Third World*, The Macmillan Press, London 1979.

Gouldner, A. (1979):   *The future of intellectuals and the rise of the new class*, The Macmillan Press, London, 1979.

Gutkind, P. (1962):   'The African urban milieu', *Civilisations*, 12, 1962, 167-91.

Gutkind, P., Cohen R. and Copans, J. (eds) (1978):   *African Labour History*, Sage Publications, Beverley Hills & London, 1978.

Gutterdige, W. (1975):   *Military Regimes in Africa*, Methuen & Co., London 1975.

Hall, J. (1962):   'Feudalism in Japan', *Comparative Studies in Society and History* 5, 1962, 15-51.

Halliday, F. and Molyneux, M. (1981):   *The Ethiopian Revolution*, Verso and New Left Books, London 1981.

Halpern, M. (1963):   *The politics of social change in the Middle East and North Africa*, Princeton University Press, Princeton 1963.

Haugen, E. (1966):   'Dialect, language, nation', *American Anthropologist* 68, 1966, 922-35.

Heller, J. (n.d.):   *Moses Hess*, The Narod Press, London.

Herbert, R. (1972):   *David, Voltaire, Brutus and the French Revolution*, Allen Lane, London 1972.

Hertzberg, A. (ed) (1960):   *The Zionist Idea, A Reader*, Meridian Books, New York 1960.

Hess, R. (1966):   'Ethiopia', in G. Carter (ed): *National Unity and Regionalism in eight African states*, Cornell University Press, Ithaca 1966.

Hilferding, R. (1910):   *Das Finanzkapital*, Marx-Studien, Vol. III, Verlag der Wiener Volksfuchhandlung, Vienna 1923; trans. E. Bass and D. Adam.

Hindess, B. & Hirst, P. (1975): *Pre-capitalist modes of production*, Routledge and Kegan Paul, London 1975.

Hobsbawm, E. (ed) (1964): *Karl Marx, Pre-capitalist Economic Formations*, Introduction, Lawrence and Wishart, London 1964.

Hobsbawm, E. (1977): 'Some reflections on "The Break-up of Britain" ', *New Left Review* 105, 1977, 3-23.

Hobson, J.A. (1902): *Imperialism, A Study*, Nisbet, London 1902.

Hodgkin, T. (1956): *Nationalism in colonial Africa*, Muller, London 1956.

Hodgkin, T. (1961): 'A note on the language of African nationalism', *St. Antony's Papers* 10, 1961, 22-40.

Hodgkin, T. (1964): 'The relevance of "Western" ideas in the derivation of African nationalism', in J.R. Pennock (ed): *Self-government in modernising societies*, Prentice-Hall, Englewood Cliffs 1964.

Hopkins, A.G. (1977): 'Imperial business in Africa', *Journal of African History* XVII/1, 1977, 29-48/2 267-90.

Hopkins, K. (1966): 'Civil-military relations in developing countries', *British Journal of Sociology* XVII, 1966, 165-82.

Hoselitz, B. and Moore, W.E. (eds) (1963): *Industrialisation and Society*, Mouton, The Hague 1963.

Hunter, G. (1962): *The new societies of Tropical Africa*, Oxford University Press, London 1962.

Huntington, S. (1968): *Political Order in Changing societies*, Yale University Press, New Haven 1968.

Jacoby, H. (1973): *The bureaucratisation of the world*, trans. E. Kanes, University of California Press, Berkeley & Los Angeles 1973.

Janowitz, M. (1964): *The military in the political development of new nations*, University of Chicago Press, Chicago & London 1964.

Johnson, C. (1962): *Peasant nationalism and communist power; the emergence of revolutionary China, 1937-45*, Stanford University Press, Stanford 1962.

Johnson, C. (1969): 'Building a communist nation in China', in R.A. Scalapino (ed): *The Communist Revolution in Asia*, Prentice-Hall, Englewood Cliffs 1969.

July, R. (1967): *The origins of modern African thought*, Faber & Faber, London 1968.

Kautsky, J.H. (ed) (1962):   *Political Change in underdeveloped countries*, John Wiley, New York 1962.

Kautsky, J.H. (1968):   *Communism and the politics of development*, John Wiley, New York 1968.

Kedourie, E. (1960):   *Nationalism*, Hutchinson, London 1960.

Kedourie, E. (1966):   *Afghani and Abduh*, Cass, London & New York, 1966.

Kedourie, E. (ed) (1971):   *Nationalism in Asia and Africa*, Weidenfeld & Nicolson, London 1971.

Kemilainen, A. (1964):   *Nationalism, Problems concerning the word, the concept and classification*, Kustantajat Publishers; Yvaskyla 1964.

Kiernan, V. (1976):   'Nationalist movement and social classes', in A.D. Smith (1976).

Kilson, M. (1958):   'The analysis of African nationalism', *World Politics* 10, 1958, 484–92.

Kilson, M. (1963):   'Authoritarian and single-party tendencies in African politics', *World Politics* 15, 1963, 262–94.

Kilson, M. (1970):   'The emergent elites of Black Africa, 1900–60', in P. Duignan & L.H. Gann (eds): *Colonialism in Africa, 1870-1960*, vol. II, Cambridge University Press, Cambridge 1970.

Kimble, D. (1963):   *A Political History of Ghana: The rise of Gold Coast nationalism, 1850-1928*, Clarendon Press, Oxford 1963.

King, P. (1976):   'Tribe: conflicts in meaning and usage', *The West African Journal of Sociology and Political Science* ½, 1976, 186–94.

Kitching, G. (1980):   *Class and Economic Change in Kenya*, Yale University Press, New York & London (1980).

Klerk, W. de. (1975):   *The Puritans in Africa*, Penguin, Harmondsworth 1975.

Kohn, H. (1955):   *Nationalism, its meaning and history*, van Nostrand, Princeton 1955.

Kohn, H. (1957):   *American nationalism*, Macmillan, New York 1957.

Kohn, H. (1957a):   *Nationalism and Liberty; the Swiss example*, Macmillan, New York 1957.

Kohn, H. (1965):   *The Mind of Germany*, Macmillan, London 1965.

Koht, H. (1947):   'The dawn of nationalism in Europe', *American Historical Review* 52, 1947, 265–80.

Kolarz, W. (1954):   *Peoples of the Soviet Far East*, Philip, London 1954.

Laclau, E. (1971):	'Imperialism in Latin America', *New Left Review* 67, 1971, 19-38.
Lanternari, V. (1965):	*The Religions of the Oppressed*, Mentor Books, New York 1965.
Lederer, I. (1969):	'Nationalism and the Yugoslavs', in Sugar & Lederer (1969).
Legum, C. (1962):	*PanAfricanism, a short political guide*, Pall Mall Press, London & Dunmow 1962.
Leiden, C. and Schmitt, K.M. (1968):	*The Politics of Violence*, Prentice-Hall, Englewood Cliffs 1968.
Lenin, V.I. (1916):	*Imperialism, the highest stage of capitalism*, Foreign Language Publishing House, Moscow 1947.
Lenin, V.I. (1920):	*Theses on the National and Colonial Questions*, in *Lenin on the National and Colonial Questions*, Foreign Language Press, Peking 1967.
Lenin, V.I. (1967):	*Lenin on the National and Colonial Questions*, Foreign Language Press, Peking 1967.
Lerner, D. (1958):	*The Passing of Traditional Society*, Free Press, New York 1958.
Levy, M. (1966):	*Modernisation and the structure of societies*, Princeton University Press, Princeton 1966.
Lewis, I. (1963):	'PanAfricanism and pan-Somalism', *Journal of Modern African Studies* I, 1963.
Lewis, I. (1980):	*The modern history of Somaliland*, 2nd ed'n, Weidenfeld & Nicolson, London 1980.
Lewis, W.A. (1965):	*Politics in West Africa,* Allen & Unwin, London 1965.
Lewis, W.H. (ed) (1965):	*French-speaking Africa: the search for identity*, Walker, New York 1965.
Lichtheim, G. (1971):	*Imperialism*, Penguin, Harmondsworth 1971.
Lijphart, A. (1977):	'Political theories and the explanation of ethnic conflict in the western world; falsified predictions and plausible post-dictions', in Esman (1977).
Little, K. (1965):	*West African urbanisation*, Cambridge University Press, Cambridge 1965.
Lloyd, P.C. (ed) (1966):	*The new elites of tropical Africa*, Oxford University Press, London 1966.
Lloyd, P.C. (1967):	*Africa in social change*, Penguin, Harmondsworth 1967.
Lowenthal, R. (1962):	'The points of the compass', in J.H. Kautsky (1962).
Lyon, J. (1980):	'Marxism and ethno-nationalism in Guinea-Bissau, 1956-76', *Ethnic & Racial Studies* 3, 1980, 156-68.

Mair, L.P. (1962):   *Primitive Government*, London 1962.

Magdoff, H. (1969):   *The Age of Imperialism*, Monthly Review Press, 1969.

Mannheim, K. (1940):   *Man and society in an age of reconstruction*, Routledge & Kegan Paul, London 1940.

Mannoni, O. (1956):   *Prospero and Caliban*, Methuen, London 1956.

Maquet, J.J. (1961):   *The Premise of Inequality in Ruanda*, Oxford University Press, London 1961.

Markovitz, I.L. (1977):   *Power and Class in Africa*, Prentice-Hall, Englewood Cliffs 1977.

Marwick, A. (1974):   *War and social change in the twentieth century*, Methuen, London 1974.

Marx, K. (1967):   *Writings of the Young Marx on Philosophy and Society*, eds. K. Guddat & D. Easton, Anchor Books, New York 1967.

Marx, K. (1976):   *Capital*, vol. I, Penguin, Harmondsworth 1976.

Marx, K. & Engels, F. (1959):   *Marx and Engels, Basic writings on politics and philosophy*, ed. L.S. Feuer, Anchor Books, New York 1959.

Mason, P. (1971):   *Patterns of dominance*, Oxford University Press, London 1971.

Masur, G. (1966):   *Nationalism in Latin America*, Macmillan, New York 1966.

Mayo, P. (1974):   *The roots of identity: three national movements in contemporary European politics*, Allen Lane, London 1974.

Mazrui, A. (1966):   *Towards a Pax Africana*, Weidenfeld & Nicolson, London 1966.

Mazrui, A. (1975):   'Ethnic stratification and the military-agrarian complex: the Uganda case', in Glazer & Moynihan (1975).

McCulley, B.T. (1966):   *English education and the origins of Indian nationalism*, Smith, Gloucester, Mass. 1966.

Mercier, P. (1965):   'On the meaning of "tribalism" in Black Africa', in van den Berghe (1965).

Middleton, J. (1958):   'The political system of the Lugbara of the Nile-Congo divide', in Middleton, J. and Tait, D. (eds): *Tribes without rulers*, London 1958. (Routledge & Kegan Paul)

Minogue, K. (1967):   *Nationalism*, Batsford, London 1967.

Minogue, K. (1967a):   'Nationalism: the poverty of a concept', *European Journal of Sociology* VIII, 1967, 332-43.

Montagne, R. (1952):   'The "modern state" in Africa and Asia', *The Cambridge Journal* 5, 1952, 583-602.

Mosse, G. (1976):	'Mass politics and the political liturgy of nationalism', in E. Kamenka (ed): *Nationalism, the nature and evoltuion of an idea*, Edward Arnold, London 1976.
Murdock, G. (1959):	*Africa: Its peoples and their culture history*, London 1959.
Nadel, S.F. (1942):	*A Black Byzantium*, Oxford University Press, London 1942.
Nairn, T. (1977):	*The Break-up of Britain*, New Left Books, London 1977.
Nettl, J.P. and Robertson, R. (1968):	*International Systems and the modernisation of societies*, Faber & Faber, London 1968.
Neuberger, B. (1976):	'The African concept of balkanisation', *Journal of Modern African Studies* XIII, 1976, 523–29.
Neuberger, B. (1977):	'State and nation in African thought', *Journal of African Studies* 4, 1977, 198-205.
Nichol, D. (ed) (1969):	*Africanus Horton: the dawn of nationalism in modern Africa*, Longmans, London 1969.
Nisbet, R.A. (1965):	*The sociological tradition*, Heinemann, London 1965.
Noth, M. (1960):	*The history of Israel*, Adam and Charles Black, London 1960.
Nottingham, J. and Rosberg, C.G. (1966):	*The myth of 'Mau Mau': nationalism in Kenya*, Praeger, New York 1966.
Nurkse, R. (1961):	*Patterns of trade and development*, Basil Blackwell, Oxford 1961.
O'Brien, P.J. (1975):	'A critique of Latin American theories of dependency', in Oxaal et al. (1975).
Olorunsola, V. (1972):	*The politics of cultural subnationalism in Africa*, Anchor Books, New York 1972.
Osborne, M. (1971):	*Region of revolt: focus on southeast Asia*, Penguin, Harmondsworth 1971.
Ottenberg, S. & P. (1960):	*Cultures and societies of Africa*, Random House, New York 1960.
Owen, R. & Sutcliffe, B. (eds) (1972):	*Studies in the Theory of Inperialism*, Longman, London 1972.
Oxaal, I., Barnett, T. and Booth, D. (eds) (1975):	*Beyond the sociology of development*, Routledge & Kegan Paul, London 1975.

Panter-Brick, S.K. (ed) (1970): *Nigerian politics and military rule*, Athlone Press, London 1970.

Parsons, T. (1961): 'Some considerations on the theory of social change', *Rural Sociology* 26, 1961, 219-39.

Parsons, T. (1966): *Societies, evolutionary and comparative perspectives*, Prentice-Hall, Englewood Cliffs 1966.

Peace, A. (1975): 'The Lagos Proletariat: Labour aristocrats of populist militants?' In Sandbrook & Cohen 1975.

Peacock, J.L. (1966): 'Religion, Communications and modernisation; a Weberian critique of some recent views', *Human Organisation* 28, 1966, 35-41.

Petersen, W. (1975): 'On the subnations of Western Europe', in Glazer and Moynihan (1975).

Pipes, R. (1975): 'Reflections of the nationality problems in the Soviet Union', in Glazer & Moynihan.

Poggi, G. (1978): *The development of the modern state*, Hutchinson & Co., London 1978.

Polk, W. (1965): 'The nature of modernisation: the Middle East and North Africa', *Foreign Affairs* 44, 1965, 100-110.

Ranger, T. (1979): 'White presence and power in Africa', *Journal of African History* XX, 1979, *passim*.

Richards, A. (1940): 'The political system of the Bemba tribe — Northeastern Rhodesia', in Fortes and Evans-Pritchard (1940).

Robinson, R. and Gallagher, J. (1961): *Africa and the Victorians*, St Martin's, New York 1961.

Roff, W. (1967): *The origins of Malay nationalism*, Yale University Press, New Haven 1967.

Rosberg, C. & Callaghan, T.M. (eds) (1979): *Socialism in Sub-Saharan Africa,* California University, Berkeley 1979.

Rodolsky, R. (1964): 'Friedrich Engels und das Problem der Geschichtsloser Völker', *Archiv für Sozialgeschichte* IV, 1964, 87-282, Hanover.

Rotberg, R. (1962): 'The rise of African nationalism: the case of East and Central Africa', *World Politics* XV, 1962, 75-90.

Rotberg, R. (1967): 'African Nationalism: concept or confusion?', *Journal of Modern African Studies* IV, 1967, 33-46.

Rothschild, D. (1972): 'Ethnic inequalities in Kenya', in Olorunsola (1972).

Roxborough, I. (1976): 'Dependency theory in the sociology of development: some theoretical considerations', *The West African Journal of Sociology and Political Science*, 1. 1976, 116-33.

Rustow, D. (1967): *A World of Nations*, The Brooking Institution, Washington D.C., 1967.

Sandbrook, R. & Cohen, R. (eds) (1975): *The development of an African working class; studies in class formation and action*, Longman, London 1975.

Said, A.A. & Simmons, L.R. (eds) (1976): *Ethnicity in an International Context*, Transaction Books, New Brunswick 1976.

Saul, J. (1973): 'African socialism in one country: Tanzania' in Arrighi and Saul (1973).

Saul, J. (1979): *The State and revoltuion in East Africa*, Heinemann, London 1979.

Scalapino, R. (ed) (1969): *The communist revolution in Asia*, Prentice-Hall, Englewood Cliffs 1969.

Seton-Watson, H. (1977): *Nations and States*, Methuen, London 1977.

Seton-Watson, H. (1978): *The Imperialist revolutionaries*, Hoover Institution Press, Stanford 1978.

Shaheen, S. (1956): *The communist theory of self-determination*, van Hoeve, The Hague 1956.

Shepperson, G. (1953): 'Ethiopianism and African nationalism', *Phylon* 14, 1953, 9-18.

Shepperson, G. (1960): 'Notes on Negro American influence on African nationalism', *Journal of African History*, I, 1960, 299-312.

Shepperson, G. and Price, T. (1958): *Independent African: John Chilembwe and the origins, setting and significance of the Nysaland Native Rising of 1915*, Edinburgh University Press, Edinburgh 1958.

Shils, E. (1960): 'The intellectuals in the political development of the new states', *World Politics* 12, 1960, 329-68.

Shils, E. (1964): *Political development in the new states*, Humanities Press, New York 1964.

Silberman, C. (1964): *Crisis in Black and White*, Random House, New York 1964.

Silvert, K. (ed) (1963): *Expectant peoples: nationalism and development*, Random House, New York 1963.

Skinner, E.P. (1964): *The Mossi of the Upper Volta*, Stanford University Press, Stanford 1964.

Sklar, R. (1963): *Nigerian political parties*, Princeton University Press, Princeton 1963.

Sklar, R. (1966): 'The contribution of tribalism to nationalism in Western Nigeria', in Wallerstein (1966).

Smelser, N.J. (1968): *Essays in Sociological Explanation*, Prentice-Hall, Englewood Cliffs 1968.

Smith, A.D. (1971): *Theories of Nationalism*, Duckworth, London 1971, 2nd ed., Duckworth, London 1982.

Smith, A.D. (1973): *The Concept of Social Change*, Routledge and Kegan Paul, London & Boston 1973.

Smith, A.D. (1973a): *Nationalism*, A Trend Report and Bibliography, *Current Sociology* 21/3, 1973 Mouton, The Hague.

Smith, A.D. (1973b): 'Nationalism and religion: the role of religious reform in the genesis of Arab and Jewish nationalism', *Archives de Sociologie des Religions* 35, 1973, 23–43.

Smith, A.D. (ed) (1976): *Nationalist Movements*, Macmillan, London 1976.

Smith, A.D. (1979): *Nationalism in the Twentieth Century*, Martin Robertson, Oxford 1979.

Smith, A.D. (1981): *The Ethnic Revival*, Cambridge University Press, Cambridge 1981.

Smith, M.G. (1960): *Government in Zazzau, 1800-1950*, Oxford University Press, London 1960.

Smythe, H.& M (1960): *The New Nigerian elite*, Stanford University Press, Stanford 1960.

Snyder, L. (1954): *The meaning of nationalism*, Rutgers University Press, New Brunswick 1954.

Staley, E. (1935): *War and the private investor*, University of Chicago Press, Chicago 1935.

Stalin, J. (1936): *Marxism and the national and colonial question*, Lawrence and Wishart, London 1936.

Steinberg, J. (1976): *Why Switzerland?*, Cambridge University Press, Cambridge 1976.

Sugar, P. (ed) (1980): *Ethnic diversity and conflict in Eastern Europe*, ABC-Clio, Santa Barbara, California 1980.

Sundkler, B.T. (1948): *Bantu Prophets in South Africa*, London 1948.

Taylor, A.J.P. (1956): *Englishmen and Others*, Hamish Hamilton, London 1956.

Taylor, J. (1979): *From modernisation to modes of production*, Macmillan, London 1979.

Thaden, E.C. (1964): *Conservative nationalism in 19th century Russia*, University of Washington Press, Seattle 1964.

Tilly, C. (ed) (1975):   *The formation of national states in Western Europe*, Princeton University Press, Princeton 1975.

Tipton, L. (ed) (1972):   *Nationalism in the Middle Ages*, Holt, Rinehart & Winston, New York 1972.

Turner, V. (1972):   'Congo-Kinshasa', in Olorunsola (1972).

Vansina, J. (1966):   *Kingdoms of the Savannah*, University of Wisconsin Press, Wisconsin 1966.

Van den Berghe, P. (ed) (1965):   *Africa: social problems of Change and conflict*, Chandler Publishing Co., San Fransisco 1965.

Vatikiotis, P. (1961):   *The Egyptian Army in Politics*, University of Indiana Press, Bloomington, Indiana 1961.

Wagner, G. (1940):   'The political organisation of the Bantu of Kavirondo', in Fortes & Evans-Pritchard (1940).

Waley, D. (1969):   *The Italian City-Republics*, World University Library, London 1969.

Wallerstein, I. (1960):   'Ethnicity and national integration in West Africa', *Cahiers d'Etudes Africaines* 3, 1960, 129-39.

Wallerstein, I. (1961):   *Africa, the politics of independence*, Vintage Books, New York 1961.

Wallerstein, I. (1965):   'Elites in French-speaking West Africa', *Journal of Modern African Studies* 3, 1965, 1-33.

Wallerstein, I. (ed) (1966):   *Social Change, the colonial situation*, John Wiley, New York 1966.

Wallerstein, I. (1967):   *Africa, the politics of unity*, Pall Mall Press, London 1967.

Wallerstein, I. (1974):   *The modern world system*, Academic Press, New York 1974.

Warren, B. (1980):   *Imperialism, Pioneer of Capitalism*, Monthly Review Press, New York and London 1980.

Weber, E. (1966):   'The men of the Archangel', *Journal of Contemporary History* I, 1966, 101-26.

Weber, M. (1947):   *From Max Weber*, ed. H. Gerth & C. Mills, Routledge and Kegan Paul, London 1947.

Weber, M. (1964):   *The theory of social and economic organisation*, ed. T. Parsons, Free Press, New York 1964.

Weber, M. (1965):   *The Sociology of Religion*, trans. E. Fischoff, Methuen, London 1965.

Weber, M. (1968): 'Ethnic Groups', in *Economy and Society*, ed. G. Roth & C. Wittich, Bedminster Press, New York 1968.

Welch, C. (1966): *Dream of unity: Pan-Africanism and political unification in West Africa*, Cornell University Press, Ithaca 1966.

Wertheim, W.F. (1956): *Indonesian society in transition*, van Hoeve, The Hague 1956.

Wilson, H.S. (ed) (1969): *The origins of West African nationalism*, Macmillan, London 1969.

Wolf, E.R. (1973): *Peasant wars of the twentieth century*, Faber & Faber, London 1973.

Worsley, P. (1964): *The Third World*, Weidenfeld & Nicolson, London 1964.

Worsley, P. (1968): *The Trumpet shall sound*, 2nd ed., McGibbon & Kee, London 1968.

Worsley, P. (1970): 'The concept of populism', in Gellner & Ionescu (1970).

Yapp, M. (1979): 'Language, religion and political identity: a general framework', in Taylor, D. & Yapp, M. (eds): *Political Identity in South Asia*, SOAS, Curzon Press, London 1979.

Young, C.M. (1965): *Politics in the Congo*, Princeton University Press, Princeton 1965.

Zernatto, G. (1944): 'Nation: the history of a word', *Review of Politics* 6, 1944, 351–66.

Zolberg, A. (1964): *One-party government in the Ivory Coast*, Princeton University Press, Princeton 1964.

Index of Names

Abidjan 44
Aborigines' Rights Protection
    Society 47
Abyssinia, see Ethiopia
Accra 44
Acheampong 131
Achimota College 45, 87
Acton, Lord 39
Aflaq, M. 105
Africa 1–3, 5, 7–8, 11–14, 16–19,
    22–5, 27–36, 37–41, 43–58,
    59–62, 64–73, 75–9, 81–93,
    96–8, 101, 106–7, 110, 112,
    114–15, 117–18, 120, 122–9,
    131–5
    – north 22–3, 35
    – west 31–3, 57, 73, 83, 92,
      115, 122
    – east 32–3, 57, 58, 89
    – central 31–2, 61
    – south 39, 115
Afrifa 129
Akwambundu 66, 119
al–Afghani 127
Alavi, H. 88–9, 90
Algeria 26, 98, 103, 106, 112
Allende 98
Allies 48
Almond, G. 4
America 9, 23, 49, 56, 77–8, 87, 106,
    110, 117–18, 122
Amhara 107
Amin 129, 131
Angola 33, 66, 97, 103, 106, 112,
    115, 117, 119, 128
Anguilla 67
Apter, D. 4
Arabs 115, 127
Argentina 23
Argyle, W.J. 67–8

Armenia 63
Ashanti 39–40, 67, 72
Ashoka 133
Asia 1, 3, 7–8, 11–14, 16–19, 23–5,
    27–30, 34–6, 38, 41, 48, 59, 60–2,
    65–6, 70–2, 76, 78–9, 81, 88, 92,
    97–8, 101–2, 122–6, 128–9, 131–5
    – central 22
    – south 27, 125
    – southeast 115, 124
Australia 12, 22, 23, 122
Austro-marxism 102
Awolowo, Chief 74
Azikiwe 49

BaKongo 27, 41–2, 64, 66–8, 119,
    125
Balanta 120
Balkans 52, 60, 73; see Yugoslavia
'Balkanisation' 24, 60
Baluchi 66
Bangla Desh 116, 128
Bannerman 46
Baroque 24
Basques 66, 100
Batista 106, 110
Bauer, O. 102
Belgium 28, 30–1, 33, 41, 45, 66, 68,
    75, 123
Bellah, R. 2
Bemba 61
Ben Bella 105, 110
Berber 91
Biafra 66, 68, 70
Bible 41, 43
Binder, L. 4–5
Blacks, Black American 43,
    54–5
Blyden, Edward 46
Bohemia, see Czechs

Bolshevik 102, 112; see communism
Brazil 12
Brew 46
Britain, –ish 9, 11, 17, 22–5, 28–33, 39, 42, 46, 51–2, 66, 71, 99, 122, 124–5
Brittany, Breton 9, 66, 100
Brussels 30
Buganda 65, 72, 127
Bulgaria 100
Burgundy 11
Burma 62, 98, 103, 124

Cabral, A. 66, 91, 105, 110, 117, 119, 120–1
Caesar 41
Cambodia 97, 103
Canada 22, 23, 78, 123
Cape Coast 47
Cape of Good Hope 23
Cape Verde 120
Caribbean 22
Casely Heyford 46, 47
Castro 105, 110
Catalonia 70
Catholicism 30, 44; see Christianity
Ceylon, see Sri Lanka
Chagga 67
Chamberlain 23
Cheikh Anta Diop 55
Chiang Kai Shek 106
Chile 98
Chilembwe, John 42
China 66, 97, 103, 105, 114–17
Christianity 14, 18, 30, 33, 41, 44, 46, 56, 91
City, of London 24
Cohen, Abner 64
Coleman, J.S. 39, 69, 73
Communist Manifesto, The 99
Congo, Congo Free State 30–1, 33, 41, 45, 66, 68, 75
Congress, of Berlin 24
Connor, Walker 11
Convention People's Party 50, 53
Copperbelt 45, 75
Copts 9, 75
Cromer, Lord 23

Crowther, Bishop 46
Cuba 98, 103, 110, 112, 115, 117
Czechs, Czechoslovakia 10, 100, 123

Dakar 44
Debray, R. 111
Denmark 123
Deutsch, K. 4, 8–11, 13
Disraeli 25
Domingo, Charles 42
Du Bois, W.E.B. 54
Durkheim, E. 59
Dutch, see Holland

East India Company 24
Egypt 9, 22, 33, 98, 106, 117
Eisenstadt, S.N. 4
Engels, F. 72, 98–100, 102, 113
England, see Britain
Epstein, A.L. 76
Eritrea 57, 65, 70, 112, 116
Ethiopia 22, 65, 67, 72, 74, 97, 103, 106–7, 112, 114–15, 117, 125, 128
'Ethiopian church' 41, 43–4
Europe 1, 10–17, 19–25, 27–30, 34–41, 43–51, 55–7, 59–60, 62, 73, 75, 77–8, 84–7, 97, 99, 101, 107, 111, 116, 123–5, 132–4
 – west 1, 11, 13–14, 37, 66, 101, 122, 124, 126
 – east 11, 55, 71, 100–3, 122–4
 – south 60
 – north 77
 – central 122
Evans-Pritchard, E. 61
Ewe 27, 57, 125

Fallers, L. 74
Fanon, F. 26
Faroes 123
Ferry 23
Fieldhouse, D.K. 25
Finland 10
First World War 42, 102
Flanders, Flemish 66
Forminière Company 30
Forster, E.M. 29

France, French 9, 11, 17, 22–5, 28, 30–3, 39, 45–7, 51–2, 70–1, 92, 99, 106, 115, 122, 124–5
French Revolution 9, 31
Freetown 45
Frisians 11
Fula 120–1

Gaels 100
Galla 65
Ganda, see Buganda
Gellner, Ernest 37, 80–1
Germany 11, 23, 24, 51, 66, 98–100, 124
Ghana 32, 39, 45, 47–8, 50, 52, 66–7, 72, 85, 131, 133
Gold Coast, see Ghana
Goody, Jack 72–3
Gouldner, A. 81
Gowon 129, 131
Great War, see First World War
Greece 9, 12, 17, 124
Guevara, Che 107, 110–11
Guinea 75, 98, 103
Guinea-Bissau 66, 97, 103, 106, 115, 117, 119–21
Gurkha 91
Gypsy 63

Habsburg 102
Haile Selassie 107
Hanseatic League 12
Harris, Wade 42
Hausa 64–5, 72, 125
Hegel, G.W.F. 100, 110
Herder, J.G. 51, 98
Hess, Moses 99
Hilferding, R. 20–1, 26
Hinduism 35
Hobson, J.A. 20, 26
Ho Chih Minh 105, 110
Hodgkin, Thomas 31, 37
Holland 11, 16–17, 28, 71, 106, 122
Horton, Africanus 46
Hungary 100, 123–4
Hunter, G. 82
Huntington, S. 111, 133
Hutu 72

Ibo 54, 64, 67–8, 74, 93
Iceland 67
India 3, 12, 22, 24, 29, 35, 62, 76, 97–8, 123, 127
Indigénat 31
Indo China 106
Indonesia 22, 62, 106, 124
Industrial Revolution 9
Iran 62
Iraq 62, 67, 98
Islam 18, 35, 91
Israel 63, 115; see Jews
Italy 12, 22, 24, 51, 100, 114
Ivory Coast 42, 45, 48

Japan 73, 105, 114
Jehovah Witnesses 43
Jerusalem, New 41–2
Jesus 41
Jews 63; see Israel

Kabyles 66,
Kakism 42
Kampala 44
Kampuchea, see Cambodia
Karen 66
Katanga 66, 70
Kautsky, J.H. 37, 79–80
Kautsky, Karl 99
Keita 98
Kenya 32, 54, 57, 64–5, 68–9, 75, 77, 89, 97, 125
Kenyatta 49, 54, 127
Kikuyu 42, 54, 57, 65, 68–9, 91, 125
Kilson, M. 74
Kimbangu, –ism 41–2
Kongo, see BaKongo
Konzo 67
Kuomintang 106
Kurds 67, 70, 91, 116

Lagos 44, 45
Lamine Gueye, Loi 31
Latin America 16–17, 22, 98, 111, 124
Legum, Colin 54
Lenin, V.I. 19–20, 25–6, 101–2, 110–11, 113, 115, 118

Leopold II 30
Leopoldville 44, 66
Lerner, D. 4–8, 76
Levy, M. 3
Liberia 41
Libya 22
Lloyd, P.C. 73
Long March 114
Luanda 115, 119
Lugbara 61
Lugusi 64
Lulua 64
Lunda 66, 70; see Katanga
Luo 54, 64, 65
Luxemburg, Rosa 101
Lyon, J. 121

Macaulay, Herbert 47
Machel 105, 110, 117
Madagascar 26
Mair, Lucy 61, 72
Malaya, –aysia 23, 62, 66, 76, 97, 124
Mali 57, 75, 98, 103, 133
Manchester Congress 54
Mandinga 67, 120–1
Manjaco 120–1
Mannheim, Karl 79
Mannoni, O. 26
Mao-Tse-Tung 105, 107, 110, 114
Maquet, J. 72
Markovitz, I.L. 74, 83–6
Marx, K. 21, 71–2, 98–100, 102, 110–11, 113, 118
Matswanism 42
Maurer, G.von 72
Mazzini 51, 98
Mengistu 112, 117
Michelet, J. 51
Middle East 5, 7, 24, 27, 35, 77, 122
Middleton, J. 61
Mill, J.S. 51–2
Mizo 66
Mobutu 129, 131
Morgan, L. 72
Moro 66
Mossi 39
Mozambique 33, 97, 103, 106, 112, 115, 117

Mugabe 117
Murdock, G.P. 61

Nadel, S.F. 72
Naga 66
Nairn, Tom 37, 53
Nairobi 44
Namibia 115
Napoleon III, Louis 25
Nasser 98, 105, 129
National Congress of West Africa 47
Negro, see Black
Négritude 55, 92
Nehru 105
Neto 105, 110, 117
New Zealand 23
Nicaragua 103
Niger 74
Nigeria 32–3, 43–5, 48, 52, 54, 65–6, 72, 74–7, 82, 85, 93, 123, 125, 128–9
Nigerian National Democratic Party 47
Nkrumah, Kwame 45, 50, 53–4, 98, 105, 127
Northern Rhodesia 32
Nuer 61
Nupe 72
Nyasaland 42
Nyerere 105

Ogaden 112, 117
Ottoman empire 16, 63, 73
Ovimbundu 66, 119

Padmore, George 54
Pakistan 62, 88–9, 124, 128
Palestine 66, 116
PanAfricanism 38, 50–1, 54–5, 92, 93
PanArabism 38
Pan-Negroism 43, 46; see Pan-Africanism
Paris 31, 92
Pathan 66
Philippines 124
Piedmont 11

Poland 100–1, 123–4
Ponty School, William 87
Portugal 22–3, 28–30, 33, 106–7, 114, 120–1, 123
Protestantism 43; see Christianity
Prussia 11

Reform Bill of 1867 52
Renner, K. 102
Rhodesia 45, 75
Richards, A. 61
Rotberg, Robert 52
Rousseau, J-J. 51, 59, 98, 119
Ruanda 72
Russia 56, 59, 100, 102, 115–18, 122, 124

Sadat 117
Saul, J. 89
Savimbi 117
Savoy 11
Saxony 11
Scots 66, 70
Second World War 10, 30, 32, 48–9, 85, 88, 119
Sekou Toure 105
Sekyi, W.E.G. 47
Seljuk Turks 63
Senegal 31, 45, 48, 52, 66, 74, 85
Senegambians 120–1
Senghor 127
Serbia 100, 114, 119, 125
Seton-Watson, H. 122
Shaba province, see Katanga
Shan 66
Shils, E. 3, 81
Shire Highlands Rising 42
Shivji, Issa 89
Siberia 22
Sierra Leone 45, 66, 74, 85
Siyad, General 115
Slavophiles 59
Slavs 9, 100
Slovenia 100
Smelser, N.J. 3
Smith, M.G. 72
Smythe, H. & M. 82
Somalia 27, 57, 64–5, 67, 98, 103, 115, 117, 119, 124–5
Somoza 106
South Africa 23, 43, 76, 122
South Moluccans 66
South Slavs, see Yugoslavia
South Yemen 97, 103
Soviet Union, see Russia
Spain 11, 17, 22, 71, 122, 124
Sri Lanka 62, 98
St.Kitts Nevis 67
Stalin, J. 101, 118
Sudan 75, 133
Sudetenland 10
Sukarno 105
Sundkler, B.T. 41, 43
Sweden 10, 71, 122, 124
Switzerland 12, 52, 123
Syria 98, 103

Tallensi 64
Tamils 66
Tanganyika, see Tanzania
Tanzania 32, 52, 58, 67, 74, 89, 98, 103
Tembu 43
'Third World' 3, 26, 35, 37, 39, 79, 81, 97, 133; see Africa, Asia, Latin America
Tibet 66
Tigre 65
Tilak 127
Tilly, Charles 13–16
Tito 105, 110, 114
Togoland 57
Tönnies, F. 59
Tsarism 22, 100, 102; see Russia
Tunisia 75
Turkey 63
Turkmen 66
Tutsi 72

Uganda 45, 65, 67, 72, 74, 77, 89, 129
Union Minière de Haut-Katanga 30
United Native African Church 43
United States, see America
U Nu 105
Upper Volta 39, 66

Vansina, J. 61
Versailles 16
Vienna 16, 20
Vietnam 97, 103, 118, 124
Vlachs 11

Wafd 106
Wagner, G. 61
Wales, Welsh 9
Wallerstein, I. 16, 24
Watchtower 42–3
Watergate 118
Weber, Max 7, 64, 94
Wends 11
West, Western 1–2, 4–8, 11, 16–19,
    45–6, 48, 50, 55–6, 58–60, 70–1,
    74, 76, 78, 81, 88, 90, 101–2, 109,
    114, 116–18, 122–6, 132–4
West Indies 54

Westminster 32–3
Westphalia, Treaty of 16, 24
Whites 29, 47–8, 54, 92
Wolof 64
Worsley, Peter 26

Xhosa 67

Yalta 16
Yoruba 54, 64, 68, 127
Yugoslavia 100, 103, 119, 123, 125,
    132; see Balkans

Zaire 75, 77, 129, 131
Zambia 61, 75
Zaria 72
Zimbabwe 75, 115, 117
Zionism 41–3, 55
Zulu 39, 68, 91, 127

Index of Subjects

absolutism 14, 24, 34, 35, 40, 100, 122–3, 126, 132
agriculture 1, 9, 11, 33, 44, 45, 72, 77, 80, 100, 107, 118, 120
ancestry 42, 61, 63
anthropology 46, 61, 72
anti-colonialism 7, 38–9, 41–2, 55, 95, 102
assimilation 9–12, 31, 33, 45, 46, 47, 52
autonomy 14, 16, 34, 51, 64, 66, 67–8, 70, 78, 89–90, 94, 134

bourgeoisie 1, 15, 18, 23, 24, 26–7, 32, 37, 48, 57, 71, 74, 77, 79, 81, 82–6, 88–9, 99, 104–5, 108–9, 111, 119, 120, 130, 132, 134; see class
bureaucracy 1, 4, 15, 26–9, 32, 34–5, 38, 45, 47–8, 50–1, 53, 56, 58, 70, 74, 76, 81–4, 86–9, 92, 95, 97, 108, 111, 118, 120, 124–5, 128–31
business, see commerce, bourgeoisie

capitalism 2, 7, 19–24, 26, 34, 37–9, 45, 55, 56–8, 72–3, 75–6, 80, 83, 85–6, 89, 99–104, 110–11, 113
caste 29, 34–5, 46, 56, 77
chief 32, 45–6, 48, 72, 73–4, 85
citizen, –ship 31, 41, 61, 63, 95, 104, 107, 130
city, city-state 12, 15, 16, 44–5, 50, 61–2, 64–5, 73–5, 77, 108, 110, 112, 119–20, 132
class, class conflict 2, 8, 10, 12, 15, 40, 42–3, 44–5, 59, 60, 70–78, 79, 81–4, 88–90, 95, 99–102, 104–5, 109, 110–11, 119, 128, 131, 134–5
class, upper/ruling 24, 74–5, 77, 83–4, 88, 110
middle 9, 24, 44, see bourgeoisie
lower/working 9, 20, 24, 30, 31–2, 53, 57, 74–7, 79–81, 90, 96, 99, 102, 104–5, 110–12, 115, 119
colonialism 18–25, 26–38, 41–2, 47–9, 50–1, 53–6, 58–60, 69, 72, 79, 85, 87–8, 90–3, 96, 102, 105–7, 110–12, 114, 116, 118, 121, 126–7, 129, 131, 133
colour, see race
commerce 11, 15–17, 20–1, 23, 25–6, 43–5, 49, 57–8, 74, 76–7, 82–3, 85–6, 89, 99, 108, 120
communications 5, 8–10, 12–13, 35, 80
communism 72, 96, 98–9, 103–7, 109–10, 112, 114–17, 118–20
community 8–9, 17, 51, 55, 59–65, 67, 69–70, 72, 76, 78, 91–7, 103–5, 109–10, 113–14, 123–7, 133, 135
culture 1–2, 6–7, 8–9, 11, 17, 27–9, 30–1, 34–6, 40, 46, 51–2, 54–6, 60–1, 63–5, 68–9, 77, 80–1, 91–6, 100–1, 108–9, 112, 120, 122–8, 133–5

democracy 21, 30, 35, 44, 47, 48, 50–3, 55, 109, 122–3, 126, 131, 134
dependency 8, 16–17, 25–6, 35, 38, 60, 106, 107, 113–14
development 1–4, 7, 10, 12, 19, 31–3, 37–9, 55, 57–9, 71, 73, 77, 80, 86, 89, 97, 99–103, 106, 110, 118–19, 126, 128–30, 132–3
diffusionism 3, 7–8
dynasty, see absolutism

economy 2, 8–9, 11, 14, 18–19, 25–6, 30, 34, 38–9, 45, 48, 50, 57, 61, 64, 70, 73, 76–7, 83–4, 89, 95, 100, 107, 111, 118, 130–1
education 5–6, 8, 10–11, 29–33, 41–2, 44–8, 52, 56–8, 74, 80–2, 84–5, 87, 90–5, 104, 107, 109, 113, 120, 130–1, 133
elite 3–4, 13, 15, 17, 19, 30–3, 38, 45–7, 50, 52–3, 56, 73–4, 76–7, 82, 84–5, 87, 90, 92, 93, 131–2
empathy 6–7
étatisme 51, 97, 129, 132
ethnicity, ethnic 8, 11, 14, 27, 40, 42–4, 46, 49–50, 52, 54, 59, 60–71, 73, 76–8, 84, 89–93, 100–2, 107, 112, 114, 116–21, 122–9, 131–2, 134–5
ethnicism/ethnocentrism 7, 65, 68–71, 77–8, 128
evolution, –ism 2–4, 62, 104

fascism 30
federalism 11, 64, 66, 78, 100, 119, 124, 135
feudalism 2, 23, 72–3, 102, 106–7, 111
'finance capital' 20–2, 102
folk, folklore 13, 109, 119
functionalism 5, 8, 62, 80

history 10–11, 13, 16–17, 36, 40–1, 52, 55, 63, 69, 71, 77, 92, 94, 100–2, 103–5, 109–11, 120, 123, 126–7, 132–3
homogenisation 6, 11–15, 34–5, 38, 50, 93, 123–4

imperialism 8, 19–22, 24–6, 30, 37–8, 55–6, 102, 105, 109–11, 113, 124
industry, –isation 7, 11–12, 20–3, 71, 76–7, 79–81, 83, 99, 110–13, 118–19
intellectuals 59, 79, 80–2, 88, 92–5, 109–10
intelligentsia 1, 3, 53, 55, 65, 74, 79–83, 85–93, 95–7, 101, 103,

105, 107–9, 113–14, 119, 121–2, 126–8, 130–5
international 16, 20, 46–7, 70, 98, 103, 113, 125, 130
irredentism 14, 65, 116

labour 20–1, 26–7, 30, 75, 77, 84–5, 99, 104
language 9–10, 12–13, 15, 51, 61, 63, 80–1, 91, 94, 120, 133
law, lawyer 31–2, 35, 46–7, 50, 82, 99, 122
liberal, –ism 21, 32, 34, 97, 129
lingua franca 13
literacy, see education

manager, –ment 4, 74–7, 85
marxism 20, 23, 65–6, 79, 84, 90, 97, 101–5, 107, 109–11, 114–17, 121
mass media 5–6, 8
migration, immigrant 9, 23, 62–4, 69, 75, 77, 122
military, –ism 15–17, 24–7, 32, 48, 59, 70, 72, 79, 82–3, 87–90, 93, 97, 100, 106–7, 111, 113–14, 128–31; see war
millennialism 37, 39; see religion
mission, –ary 18, 26, 30, 32, 41, 45, 57, 94
mobilisation 4–7, 9–12, 15–16, 37, 42, 51, 53, 62, 69, 97–8, 105–7, 109–11, 118, 120, 127–8, 131, 134
mobility 5–6, 8, 48, 63, 82, 84, 130
modernity, –isation 2–8, 12–13, 17–18, 23, 33–4, 37, 42, 74, 79–81, 107–8, 118, 130
multinational state, plural state, see federalism
multinational corporations 60, 77, 86, 111
myth 13, 40, 61, 63, 126–7

nation, nationality 1, 5, 8–14, 17, 19, 21, 40, 42–4, 46, 52–4, 56, 61, 63–4, 66–8, 71, 81, 91, 94–5, 97–102, 103–5, 110–12, 115–16, 122–3, 125–9, 131–5
nationalism 1–3, 5–7, 10–11, 19, 21,

23, 27, 32, 36, 37–58, 63–4, 67–9, 75, 80–1, 88, 90–1, 93–6, 97–121, 127, 129–30, 132, 134–5
– civic, demotic 52, 94
–cultural, linguistic 37, 94–5, 117
– ethnic 38, 65–9, 92–3, 119, 135
– marxist, communist 98, 103, 105–6, 108, 110–21
– territorial 33, 50–5, 65, 67, 69, 91–3, 117, 130–1, 135
nation-state 6, 8–11, 12–14, 21, 65, 80–1, 96, 101, 113–14
nativism 3, 41

'parallel society' 29
participation 4–7, 33, 53, 104–5, 129
party, one-party 37, 47, 49–50, 53–4, 59, 69, 74–5, 83–4, 105–6, 109, 111–13, 115, 118
paternalism 29–31, 56
peasantry 14, 31–2, 42, 45, 52–3, 72–3, 77, 80, 84, 90, 105, 107–12, 114, 119–20, 127–8, 133
periphery 2, 4, 16, 37, 42, 68, 124
'political community' 14, 49–50, 52, 69, 97, 126–8, 132–5
populism 107–9, 114–15
'post-colonial' state 48, 70–1, 82, 88–90, 93, 96, 133–4
'primary resistance' 39–41
production 2, 18, 20, 31, 34, 57–8, 73, 76, 78, 84–6, 100, 113, 128
professionals, ism 46–7, 74, 82–5, 87–90, 93–5, 107–9, 113, 129–30, 133–4

race, –ism 7, 21, 26, 29–30, 46–8, 54, 69, 90–2, 98
religion 5, 7, 13, 15, 18, 35, 37, 41–4, 46, 63, 91, 119
revolution 9, 81, 98–9, 101–2, 104, 109–11, 115, 117, 120

secession, separatism 14, 43–4, 54, 65–7, 70, 80, 94, 102, 112, 116, 128
settlers 26, 32–3, 89, 92
slavery 18, 55, 73
socialism 3, 32, 74, 80, 97–9, 101–3, 105–6, 109–10, 112–13, 115–18; see marxism, communism
state 1–5, 7, 9–17, 19, 21, 24–7, 32, 34–6, 50–1, 54, 56, 58–60, 64, 66–9, 70–4, 76, 79–81, 84, 86–92, 94–5, 97, 100–2, 105–7, 111–12, 116–19, 122–35
– 'inter-state' system 16, 19, 23–5, 27, 34, 71, 90, 116–17, 134

territory, territorialism 14–17, 19, 22–5, 27–30, 32, 35, 38, 47, 49–52, 56, 58, 60–1, 63–5, 69, 87, 90–1, 93, 95, 97, 99, 105, 110, 112–13, 116, 118–20, 122–35
trade, see commerce
tradition, –alism 2, 4–7, 9, 11, 18, 28, 32–4, 39, 46, 48, 62, 65, 74, 80, 108, 112, 116, 119, 126–8
tribe, –alism 14, 18–19, 23, 40, 46, 49, 54, 60–9, 72–8, 85, 91, 114–15, 118, 121, 125, 127, 132

union, trades 12, 37, 53, 60, 75–6, 85, 108, 115
university 46, 82, 87, 120; see education
urbanisation 1, 5–6, 10–12, 17–18, 45, 57, 61, 64–5, 69, 93, 107–8; see city
– urban associations 49, 69, 74

westernisation 3–4, 7, 80, 130, 132
war 14–16, 19, 25, 39–40, 48–9, 56, 60–1, 66, 68, 70, 73, 91, 104–5, 107, 110–11, 114–15, 117, 119–20, 124